The Power of Prophetic Decrees and Declarations: Unlocking Heaven

Speak Life, Command Blessings, and Transform Your World Through the Authority of God's Word

Dr. Angelina Onuzulike

contained within this document, including, but not limited to, errors, omissions, or inaccuracies.

Table of Contents

Biblical References: All biblical references in this book are sourced from the New King James Bible (2017).

Introduction

Thou shalt also decree a thing, and it shall be established unto thee:
and the light shall shine upon thy ways. –Job 22:28

Words are more than mere sounds or symbols. They carry power, influence, and authority. From the beginning, God demonstrated the transformative power of spoken words, creating the heavens and the heart with divine commands. That same creative power is available to believers today through prophetic decrees and declarations. These are not empty rituals but spiritual principles rooted in Scripture, capable of shaping realities and bringing God's will into manifestation.

Prophetic decrees are more than words spoken in prayer. They are faith-filled declarations that align with God's Word. When we decree something in agreement with Scripture, we activate spiritual laws and release God's power to operate in our lives. This concept is grounded in biblical truth. In Genesis, God created the world by speaking it into existence. He said, "Let there be light," and light appeared.

This same authority is extended to believers. Proverbs 18:21 says, "Death and life are in the power of the tongue." The words we speak shape the outcomes we experience. A prophetic decree is not a wish or a casual statement but a proclamation of God's promises, spoken with confidence and faith.

Consider the story of the centurion in Matthew 8:8. He told Jesus, "...but speak the word only, and my servant shall be healed." His faith in the power of spoken words brought immediate healing. This example demonstrates that when words are spoken in alignment with God's will, they carry the authority of heaven.

Why Decrees Are Significant

Prophetic decrees are essential for every believer because they bridge the gap between God's promises and our reality. Many Christians know God's Word but struggle to see it manifest in their lives. This often happens because they fail to activate those promises through faith and declaration.

When you decree healing, provision, or breakthrough, you are actively partnering with God to bring His plans to fruition. This act of speaking life into situations is not just a practice of faith, it's a demonstration of authority. As co-heirs with Christ, we have been given the privilege of declaring His will on earth as it is in heaven, as found in Romans 8:17, "And if children, then heirs; heirs of God, and joint heirs with Christ; if so be that we suffer with him, that we may be also glorified together." And in Matthew 6:10, "Thy kingdom come. Thy will be done on earth, as it is in heaven."

In this book, you will find guidance to understand and apply the principles of prophetic decrees. You will learn the following:

- **The Biblical foundation of decrees:** Explore how God's Word supports the practice of declarations.

- **How to craft effective decrees:** Discover the key elements of faith-filled proclamations.

- **Practical application:** Learn how to use decrees in areas such as health, finances, relationships, and spiritual growth.

- **Spiritual warfare:** Equip yourself with declarations to overcome fear, doubt, and opposition.

- **Testimonies of breakthroughs:** Be inspired by real-life stories of lives transformed through prophetic declarations.

By the end of this book, you will be equipped to use the power of your words to align with God's will and experience His promises in every area of your life.

Faith is the key that unlocks the power of prophetic decrees. Without faith, words remain empty. Hebrews 11:6 says, "But without faith, it is impossible to please him." Prophetic decrees are not about repeating phrases but about speaking with a heart full of belief in God's promises.

Faith sees the outcome before it happens. When you decree healing, faith envisions the restoration of health. When you declare provision, faith trusts in God's abundance even before it manifests. Unwavering belief transforms ordinary words into spiritual weapons.

About the Author

I am Dr. Angelina Onuzulike, and my life is a testament to the power of faith and prophetic declarations. With a doctorate in Christian Philosophy and Divinity, as well as Nursing leadership and Management, I bring both spiritual depth and practical insight to my work.

I have spent decades teaching believers how to use their God-given authority to transform their lives through declarations. My journey has been one of personal breakthroughs, divine encounters, and a deep passion for helping others discover the power of God's Word. Through my ministry, books, and teachings, I have equipped thousands to walk in the promises of God.

My dual expertise in theology and healthcare gives me a unique perspective on the holistic impact of prophetic decrees. I understand the spiritual, emotional, and physical dimensions of transformation and bring the understanding into every word I share.

Throughout Scripture, words have been used to create, heal, and restore. In Ezekiel 37, God commands the prophet to speak to the valley of dry bones. As Ezekiel obeyed, the bones came to life, forming a vast army. The power was not in Ezekiel himself but in the spoken Word of God.

This example illustrates the essence of prophetic decrees. When we speak God's Word, we release His creative power into our circumstances. Dry bones represent situations that seem hopeless, yet through decrees, they can be revived.

Decrees as Spiritual Weapons

Life is a spiritual battlefield. Ephesians 6:12 reminds us, "For we wrestle not against flesh and blood, but against principalities, against powers, against the rulers of the darkness of this world, against spiritual wickedness in high places." Prophetic decrees are a powerful weapon in this battle.

When fear, doubt, or opposition arises, decrees allow us to stand firm in faith. By declaring, "For God hath not given us the spirit of fear, but of power, and of love, and a sound mind," 2 Timothy 1:7 shifts the atmosphere and drives out fear. Similarly, decrees of provision, healing, or restoration reinforce God's promises in the face of adversity.

This book balances theory and transformation. Each chapter builds on the foundation of prophetic decrees, systematically guiding you to apply these principles to your life.

You will learn to identify areas where God's promises need to be activated, craft declarations rooted in Scripture, and consistently speak life over your circumstances. This journey will deepen your faith and empower you to walk in victory.

As you start, remember that the power of prophetic decrees lies in their alignment with God's Word. They are not magical incantations. They are acts of faith rooted in the authority of Scripture.

Your voice matters. It has the power to shape your reality, influence your future, and align your life with God's will. Through this book, you will learn to wield that power with confidence and wisdom.

The time to speak life into our existence is now. Step into the authority God has given you, and watch as your declarations bring light into darkness, order into chaos, and victory into every challenge.

Chapter 1:

The Biblical Foundation of

Prophetic Decrees

Death and life are in the power of the tongue: and they that love it shall eat the fruit thereof. –Proverbs 18:21

Words have power. They shape our lives, influence our choices, and reveal our faith. Proverbs 18:21 reminds us of the incredible responsibility we hold with our words: They can bring life or destruction. This principle is central to prophetic decrees, where we intentionally align our speech with God's Word to manifest His will in our lives.

This chapter explores the biblical foundation of decrees. We'll examine how figures in both the Old and New Testaments used the authority of spoken words to bring about divine outcomes. Through their examples, we'll learn how to wield this authority. Let's begin by looking at some key Old and New Testament passages and how they shape our understanding of decrees.

Scriptural Basis for Decrees

Using Scripture in prophetic decrees is a powerful practice that aligns our words with God's truth. When we declare God's promises over our lives, we are not merely speaking positive affirmations but engaging with His eternal Word. The Bible is living and active as declared in Hebrews 4:12, "For the Word of God is quick, and powerful, and sharper than any two-edged sword, piercing even to the dividing asunder of soul and spirit, and of the joints and marrow, and is a discerning of the thoughts and intents of the heart." When we speak it out loud, we release its transformative power into our circumstances. This practice allows us to claim the truths and promises that God has already established.

Scripture provides both authority and clarity in our decrees. On our own, our words may lack strength or direction, but when rooted in God's Word, they carry divine power. Using Scripture in our decrees, we remind ourselves and declare to the spiritual realm what God has already spoken. For example, Philippians 4:19 reinforces trust in God's provision and invites His intervention in times of financial strain: "And my God shall supply all your need according to His riches in glory by Christ Jesus."

Including Scripture in our decrees also builds our faith. Romans 10:17 states that faith comes by hearing, and hearing by the Word of God. Each time we declare Scripture, we are reminded of God's character and His faithfulness. This repetition strengthens our belief and realigns our hearts with His will. In doing so, we position ourselves to receive the fullness of His blessings and walk in the authority He has given us.

Old Testament Examples

Job 22:28: "You will also decree a thing, and it will be established for you; so light will shine on your ways."

This verse from Job introduces the principle of declaring truth into reality. It emphasizes partnership with God. The phrase "declare a thing, and it will be established for you" shows us how words spoken in faith lead to divine action.

Take, for example, the story of Abraham. God promised him descendants as numerous as the stars. In Genesis 17:5, God declared, "No longer shall your name be called Abram, but your name shall be Abraham; for I have made you a father of many nations." God's declaration came long before the promise was fulfilled. Abraham embraced it, calling himself by this new name even when the circumstances seemed impossible.

Abraham's faith mirrors the principle in Job 22:28. He aligned his words with God's decree, and the promise came to pass in time. His story reminds us that declaring God's truth over our lives isn't about denying reality but trusting His Word above all else.

Numbers 6:22–27 "And the Lord spoke to Moses, saying: 'Speak to Aaron and his sons, saying, 'This is the way you shall bless the children of Isreal. Say to them: The Lord bless you and keep you; The Lord make His face shine upon you, and be gracious to you; the Lord lift up His countenance upon you, and give you peace. So they shall put My name on the children of Israel, and I will bless them."

These words weren't mere niceties. They carried divine authority. When the priests spoke this blessing, they invoked God's presence, protection, and peace over the people.

A modern parallel can be seen in families who pray blessings over their children. A mother might declare, "You are loved, chosen, and blessed by God. You will grow in wisdom and grace." These words, spoken consistently, shape a child's identity and confidence. Studies on positive affirmations support this biblical truth, showing that words spoken over others impact their mental and emotional well-being (Sara, 2022).

This priestly blessing is a profound example of decrees in action. In this passage, God instructs Moses to tell Aaron and his sons to bless the Israelites. In both Job 22:28 and Numbers 6:22–27, we see a recurring theme: Declarations spoken in alignment with God's will bring spiritual and practical transformation.

New Testament Foundations

In the New Testament, Jesus expands the concept of decrees, teaching His disciples about binding and loosing: "...whatever you loose on earth will be loosed in heaven," as found in Matthew 18:18.

This verse establishes the believer's authority to declare God's will on earth. *Binding* represents forbidding something while *letting loose* permits it. Both actions require faith and alignment with God's purposes.

A relatable example is the act of praying for protection over a home. A family might declare, "We bind every spirit of fear or strife in this house and let loose God's peace and love." When you speak these words over your home, you exercise spiritual authority, inviting heaven's intervention.

Research into the psychology of belief shows the power of speaking positive intentions. A study published in the Journal of Behavioral Medicine found that individuals who verbalize faith-based affirmations experience lower stress and higher resilience (Papaleontiou-Louca, 2021). This highlights the truth of Matthew 18:18: "Assuredly, I say to you, whatever you bind on earth will be bound in heaven, and whatever you loose on earth will be loose in heaven."

Romans 4:17 describes God as the one who "calls those things which do not exist as though they did." This principle of speaking things into existence is tied to Abraham's story. Despite his advanced age and Sarah's barrenness, Abraham believed in God's promise. He spoke and lived as if the promise was already fulfilled.

This kind of faith-filled declaration doesn't ignore reality; it celebrates God's power to transform it. A modern example is found in testimonies of healing. A woman battling cancer might declare daily, "By His stripes, I am healed" as found in Isaiah 53:5. While undergoing treatment, she aligns her words with God's promises, holding on to faith for her healing.

Testimonies like these abound in Christian communities. One such example found in Guidepost magazine frequently shares stories of individuals who experience breakthroughs through faith-filled declarations (Johnson, n.d.).

Consider the story of the Johnson family, who faced financial difficulties. With mounting bills and limited income, they felt overwhelmed. Instead of succumbing to fear, they turned to God's promises. They began declaring Philippians 4:19 daily: "And my God shall supply all your need according to His riches in glory by Christ Jesus."

Each morning, the family would gather for prayer, thanking God for His provision. They decreed, "We are not lacking because God is our provider. Doors of opportunity are opening for us."

Weeks later, unexpected blessings began to unfold. Mr. Johnson received a promotion, and a neighbor offered free childcare, reducing their expenses. The family created these changes through their declarations of faith, which aligned their hearts with God's promises.

The Authority of the Believer

Authority in the life of a believer is not a distant concept; it is a cornerstone of Christian faith. When Jesus ascended to heaven, He allowed His followers to continue His work on earth. This authority is not earned by personal merit and can only be granted through our relationship with Him. It is a divine gift that empowers us to act as His representatives, carrying out His will in our lives and the world around us.

When you understand your spiritual authority, you recognize that you are not powerless in the face of life's challenges. Through Christ, you are equipped to stand firm, speak boldly, and overcome obstacles. Luke 10:19 reminds us of this: "Behold, I give you the authority to trample on serpent and scorpions, and over all the power of the enemy, and nothing shall by any means hurt you." These words show us the profound truth that God has entrusted believers with His power to resist evil, declare His promises, and bring His kingdom to earth.

Living with authority does not mean avoiding hardship or struggle. Instead, it means we can face trials with confidence, knowing we are not alone. The believer's authority allows us to approach life with the assurance that God is working through us, guiding and equipping us for every challenge.

Understanding Your Spiritual Authority in Christ

Have you ever felt powerless in the face of a daunting situation? Perhaps it was a sudden health crisis, a broken relationship, or a financial burden. These moments can leave us feeling small, overwhelmed, and lost. But as a child of God, you are never without hope or power.

In Christ, your spiritual authority is rooted in His victory on the cross. Jesus' death and resurrection defeated sin, death, and the forces of darkness. Through Him, you have been given the authority to stand firm against any attack, to declare His promises over your life, and to walk confidently in His purpose. Ephesians 2:6 says, "And raised us up together, and made us sit together in the heavenly places in Christ Jesus." This means that, as believers, we share in Christ's authority and position.

To understand this better, consider how earthly authority works. Imagine a police officer directing traffic. The officer's authority does not come from personal strength but from the badge that represents the law they serve. Similarly, your autonomy comes not from your abilities but from Christ who works through you. When you speak His Word, heaven backs you up.

One powerful way to exercise this authority is through prayer and declarations. For instance, if you are battling anxiety, you can declare 2 Timothy 1:7 "For God has not given us a spirit of fear, but of power and of love and of a sound mind." When speaking this truth, you are aligning your mind and heart with God's promises and resisting the lies that fear tries to impose.

Walking in spiritual authority also includes understanding the power of your identity. You are a child of God, chosen and dearly loved.

When challenges come, remind yourself of who you are in Him. Speak truths like Romans 8:37 over your life: "Yet in all these things we are more than conquerors through Him who loved us."

It is also important to act on this authority. Just as soldiers are trained to use their equipment, you must be intentional about applying God's Word in your daily life. Study the Scriptures, seek guidance through prayer, and step out in faith, knowing that God has equipped you for every good work.

Spiritual authority is not arrogance or self-reliance. It is about humility and dependence on Christ. It is knowing that apart from Him, we can do nothing as advised in John 15:1: "I am the vine, you are the branches. He who abides in Me, and I in him, bears much fruit; for without Me you can do nothing." But in Him, we can do all things as found in Philippians 4:13: "I can do all things through Christ who strengthens me." Whatever you face today, remember this: You are not fighting alone, and you are not fighting without power. God has given you everything you need to walk in victory.

How to Wield That Authority Effectively

Your first step is to understand that you have spiritual authority in Christ. But knowing how to use that authority effectively is just as important. Like a skilled artisan must learn to handle their tools, so must you learn to wield the authority given to you by God. This involves faith, intentionality, and a deep connection with Him. Here are some strategies to help you effectively walk in and experience your God-given authority.

Stay Rooted in God's Word

The Bible is your foundation. It is the source of truth and power, equipping you to stand firm in any situation. Hebrews 4:12 reminds us that the Word of God is a double-edged sword. To wield your authority, you must first know what God's Word says about who you are and what you have been given.

If you are praying for healing, you can declare verses like Isaiah 53:5. If you are battling fear, you can speak Psalm 27:1 over your life: "The Lord is my light and my salvation; whom shall I fear? The Lord is the strength of my life; of whom shall I be afraid?" Familiarize yourself with Scriptures that apply to your circumstances. Memorize them, meditate on them, and let them guide your prayers and declarations.

Imagine facing a stressful financial situation. Instead of succumbing to worry, you could declare Philippians 4:19. Speak this verse with confidence, believing in God's provision even when you cannot see it yet.

Develop a Strong Prayer Life

Prayer is one of the most powerful ways to wield spiritual authority. Through prayer, you align yourself with God's will and invite His power into your life. James 5:16 says, "Confess your trespasses to one another and pray for one another, that you may be healed. The effective, fervent prayer of a righteous man avails much." Prayer is not passive; it is active, intentional communication with God.

When you pray, speak boldly. Approach God with faith, not timidity, as Hebrews 4:16 encourages: "Let us, therefore, come boldly to the throne of grace, that we may obtain mercy and find grace to help in time of need." Pray specific prayers, standing on Scripture as your foundation. Declare God's promises over your life, your family, and your circumstances.

Practical strategy: Begin each day by praying over key areas of your life:

- Over your health: Declare healing and strength—Psalm 103:3.

- Over your family: Pray for unity and protection—Psalm 91:11.

- Over your work: Ask for wisdom and favor—James 1:5.

Speak With Authority

Words carry power. Proverbs 18:21, "Death and life are in the power of the tongue, and those who love it will eat its fruit." When you speak, let your words align with God's truth rather than your fears or doubts. Avoid negative speech that contradicts what you believe in.

Speaking with authority does not mean being loud or aggressive; it means speaking with conviction. Declare God's promises over your life and your loved ones with faith that they will come to pass. For example, when faced with challenges, declare Philippians 4:13: "I can do all things through Christ who strengthens me."

A parent whose child is struggling in school might say, "I believe God has given my child the mind of Christ. They are fearfully and wonderfully made and capable of great things." 1 Corinthians 2:16: "For who has known the mind of the Lord that he may instruct Him?" But we have the mind of Christ: Psalm 139:14, "I will praise You, for I am fearfully and wonderfully made; Marvelous are Your works, and that my soul knows very well."

Stand Firm Against Opposition

Walking in authority does not mean you will not face challenges. In fact, the enemy often seeks to undermine your confidence in God's promises. Ephesians 6:13 instructs, "Therefore take up the whole armor of God, that you may be able to withstand in the evil day, and having done all, to stand."

When opposition arises, refuse to back down. Stand firm in your faith, declaring God's Word and resisting the enemy's lies. James 4:7 says, "Therefore submit to God. Resist the devil and he will flee from you."

When you encounter fear, doubt, or discouragement, remind yourself of God's faithfulness. Keep a journal of answered prayers and victories to revisit during difficult times.

Partner With the Holy Spirit

The Holy Spirit is your guide, teacher, and source of power. Relying on Him is essential for wielding spiritual authority effectively. Romans 8:26 reminds us, "Therefore submit to God. Resist the devil and he will flee from you." When you are unsure how to pray or act, ask the Holy Spirit to lead you.

Listen to the Holy Spirit by quieting distractions and spending time in His presence. As you grow in sensitivity to His voice, you will find greater confidence in your decisions and actions.

If you feel prompted to pray for someone but are unsure what to say, simply start and trust the Holy Spirit to guide your words. Often, He will bring specific Scriptures or insights to mind as you pray.

Walk in Obedience

Authority is linked to obedience. When you align your actions with God's Word, you position yourself to operate in His power. Disobedience weakens your authority, but obedience strengthens it. Examine your life regularly. Ask God to reveal any areas where you need to align more closely with His will. Whether forgiving someone, stepping out in faith, or letting go of a harmful habit, obedience opens the door for God's authority to flow through you.

Wielding your authority effectively is about faith, persistence, and a heart surrendered to God. As you grow in understanding and application, you will see His power at work in your life. Remember, this authority is not yours alone but a gift from Christ.

Whatever challenges you face, know that you are not powerless. Stand tall, speak boldly, and trust that God's promises are true. You have been given authority to thrive in and make a lasting impact on His kingdom.

As we reflect on the authority God has entrusted to us, it becomes clear that this authority is not meant to be dormant. It is activated and exercised through our actions and, perhaps most powerfully, our words. From creation itself, where God spoke the universe into existence, to Jesus declaring healing, peace, and freedom, the power of the spoken word is evident throughout Scripture. Let's look deeper into this divine truth and discover how your words can become tools of victory and vessels of God's power.

Chapter 2:

The Power of the Spoken Word

For assuredly, I say to you, whoever says to this mountain, 'Be removed and be cast into the sea,' and does not doubt in his heart, but believes that those things he says will be done, he will have whatever he says. —Mark 11:23

Words are not just sounds; they are vessels of power. From the very beginning, words have played a central role in creation and transformation. God spoke, and the universe came into existence. Jesus spoke, and storms calmed, diseases fled, and lives were restored. The Bible teaches us that our words carry weight. They can create, heal, and build and destroy, hurt, and tear down.

As believers, the power of the spoken word is a divine gift and a responsibility. The words you choose to speak reflect the condition of your heart and your level of faith. They shape your reality and influence the world around you. By aligning your words with God's truth, you activate His promises and release His power into your life and circumstances.

The Creative Power of Words

Words have creative potential. This truth is not just poetic—it is deeply spiritual and foundational. Genesis 1 reveals a profound reality that God created the world by speaking it into existence: Genesis 1:3,

"Then God said, 'Let there be light'; and there was light." Every word spoken by God carried life and purpose, transforming void and chaos into order and beauty.

As beings made in His image, we share in His ability to create with our words: Genesis 1:27, "So God created man in His own image; in the image of God He created him; male and female He created them." While we do not wield the infinite power of God, our words still carry significant spiritual and emotional influence. Think of how a kind word can brighten someone's day or how harsh criticism can leave lasting scars. The creative power of words is a tool God has entrusted to us for His glory and the good of others.

Proverbs 18:21 highlights the power of words: "Death and life are in the power of the tongue, and those who love it will eat its fruit." This verse speaks to the dual capacity of words to build up or tear down. When we use words intentionally and wisely, they can inspire hope, ignite faith, and lead others to Christ. However, when used carelessly or in anger, words can wound, discourage, and push people away.

Consider everyday scenarios where words shape outcomes. A teacher's encouragement can awaken confidence in a struggling student, leading to academic success. A parent's loving affirmation can instill self-worth in a child, laying a foundation for emotional resilience. Conversely, a single word spoken in anger during an argument can fracture relationships, causing wounds that take years to heal. These everyday examples echo the spiritual principle of sowing and reaping; the words we sow into others' lives will produce either good or harmful fruit.

In a spiritual sense, words also frame our realities. Hebrews 11:3: "By faith, we understand that the worlds were framed by the Word of God so that the things which are seen were not made of things which are visible." Just as God framed the universe with His words, we can frame our personal circumstances through our speech. When our words align with God's truth, they become vessels of His creative power. Speaking Scripture over situations is not mere repetition but an act of faith that aligns our hearts with God's will and invites His power into the situation.

The creative power of words also extends to prayer and worship. When we lift our voices in praise, we declare God's goodness and affirm His sovereignty. In Acts 16:25–26: "But at midnight Paul and Silas were praying and singing hymns to God, and the prisoners were listening to them. Suddenly there was a great earthquake so that the foundations of the prison were shaken, and immediately all the doors were opened and everyone's chains were loosed." This biblical account reminds us that words spoken in faith can break chains and open doors, both physically and spiritually.

Science, too, reinforces the power of words. Studies in psychology and neuroscience have shown how positive affirmations can reshape neural pathways, improving mental health and resilience. The words we choose to speak and meditate upon rewire our brains, demonstrating the profound interplay between the spiritual and physical realms. This proves the importance of choosing words that align with God's Word, which renews the mind and transforms lives. Romans 12:2: "And do not be conformed to this world, but be transformed by the renewing of your mind, that you may prove what is that good and acceptable and perfect will of God."

The creative power of words is a divine gift, one that calls for stewardship. Ephesians 4:29: "Let no corrupt word proceed out of your mouth, but what is good for necessary edification, that it may impart grace to the hearers." This verse admonishes believers to use words that "edify and impart grace to the hearers." This guidance shows that our speech should reflect God's love and truth, building up those around us and glorifying Him. When we grasp the creative potential of our words and wield them responsibly, we participate in

God's redemptive work, bringing light into darkness and hope into despair.

Let these words inspire you to speak life boldly and intentionally. Whether through prayer, declarations, or everyday conversations, remember that your words have the power to create, heal, and transform. Use them to align with God's purposes, reflect His character, and release His blessings into the world around you.

Biblical Examples of Spoken Words Creating Change

Throughout the Bible, we see examples of how words, spoken in faith and authority, brought about miraculous changes:

- **God's words in creation:** In the beginning, God demonstrated the ultimate example of the creative power of words. He didn't work with His hands to form the universe; He spoke it into being. His words set the start of places, separated the waters, and filled the earth with life in Genesis 1:1–31.

- **Moses and the parting of the Red Sea:** When the Israelites faced the Red Sea with Pharaoh's army in pursuit, God instructed Moses to speak and act in obedience. Moses declared God's will, lifted his staff, and the sea parted, creating a path to safety as found in Exodus 14:21–22. His word and faith activated God's power to deliver His people.

- **Jesus' ministry:** In the New Testament, Jesus consistently demonstrated the power of spoken words. He calmed a raging storm with a simple command—Mark 4:39: "Peace, be still!" He spoke healing to the sick, saying, "Be cleansed," and lepers were healed instantly as found in Matthew 8:3. He even raised

Lazarus from the dead with the declaration, "Lazarus, come forth!" in John 11:43.

- **Prophetic declarations:** The prophets of old spoke God's words with authority, and their declarations shaped nations and destinies. When Ezekiel prophesied over dry bones, declaring God's life-giving words, those bones came together, and life was restored, as found in Ezekiel 37:4–10.

The Relationship Between Faith and Declaration

The power of your words is directly tied to your faith. Speaking without faith is like using an uncharged tool—it lacks the energy to produce results. Jesus emphasized this connection when He taught His disciples in Matthew 17:20: "So Jesus said to them, 'Because of your unbelief; for assuredly, I say to you, if you have faith as a mustard seed, you will say to this mountain, 'Move from here to there,' and it will move; and nothing will be impossible for you.'"

Faith fuels the effectiveness of your declarations. When you speak with confidence in God's promises, you align your words with His will. This partnership between faith and spoken words activates heaven's authority on earth.

Consider someone struggling with anxiety. They might declare, "I will not fear because God is with me," based on Isaiah 41:10. When spoken in faith, this declaration shifts their focus from fear to God's presence, inviting His peace to take over. Over time, consistent faith-filled declarations can rewire their mindset and align their emotions with God's truth.

Steps to strengthen the connection between faith and declaration:

1. **Meditate on God's Word:** Regularly immerse yourself in Scripture. This builds a reservoir of truth in your heart that will naturally flow into your declaration.

2. **Pray for increased faith:** Faith grows as you spend time with God. Ask Him to strengthen your belief in His power and promises.

3. **Speak aloud with confidence:** When making declarations, speak boldly. The authority of your words grows as you exercise it.

4. **Practice gratitude:** Thank God in advance for what He is doing through your words. Gratitude reinforces faith and keeps your focus on His faithfulness.

The connection between faith and declaration is a divine partnership. As you build on your ability to use both, you will begin to see God's power move in ways you never imagined.

The Role of Faith in Prophetic Declarations

Faith is the engine that drives the power of prophetic declarations. Without it, even the most eloquent words become hollow and ineffective. Faith is the bridge between our spoken words and God's limitless power, ensuring that what we declare aligns with His promises. Hebrews 11:6 reminds us of this promise. Faith assures us that our declarations are divine truths that activate God's plans in our lives and that they are not mere wishes.

This section explores the necessity of faith in prophetic declarations, the practical steps to align your heart and mind with God's Word, and ways to overcome doubt and unbelief. Real-life examples illustrate how faith has turned declarations into miracles, providing hope and encouragement for your journey.

Faith is essential because it connects you to God's supernatural power. When you speak in faith, you are not relying on your own strength or understanding but on the infinite capabilities of the Creator of all. This reliance empowers your words to transcend natural limitations, bringing divine intervention into human circumstances.

Faith-filled declarations remind us of the truth found in Romans 4:17, where Paul describes Abraham's faith: "...God, who gives life to the dead and calls those things which do not exist as though they did." Abraham believes in God's promise of countless descendants despite his and Sarah's advanced ages. His faith transformed a seemingly impossible situation into the foundation of God's covenant with Israel.

How to Align Your Heart and Mind With God's Word

To make effective prophetic declarations, your heart and mind must be synchronized with God's truth. This alignment ensures that your declarations reflect His will, not personal desires or fleeting emotions.

1. **Immerse yourself in Scripture:** God's Word is the foundation of every prophetic declaration. Spend time reading, meditating on, and memorizing Scripture. The more familiar you are with His promises, the more confident and accurate your declarations will be. For example, if you are struggling with provision, declare Philippians 4:19 over your challenges.

2. **Pray for guidance:** Prayer invites the Holy Spirit to reveal God's specific will for your situation. As you seek Him, He will guide your thoughts and shape your declarations to align with His plans.

3. **Have a heart of obedience:** Alignment with God's Word requires submission to His authority. When you live in obedience to His commands, your declarations carry more weight because they come from a place of integrity and faithfulness.

4. **Renew your mind:** Replace negative thoughts with God's truth. Romans 12:2 encourages us: "And do not be conformed to this world but be transformed by the renewing of your mind..." When your mind is renewed, your declarations flow naturally from a place of faith and assurance.

Overcoming Doubt and Unbelief

Doubt and unbelief are common obstacles that can hinder the effectiveness of prophetic declarations. Even the most faithful believers face moments of uncertainty, but overcoming these barriers is crucial for unlocking the full potential of your words.

1. **Recognize the source of doubt:** Doubt often stems from fear, past disappointments, or a lack of understanding of God's promises. By identifying the root cause, you can address it with Scripture and prayer. If fear of failure is holding you back, meditate on Isaiah 41:10, "Fear not, for I am with you; be not dismayed, for I am your God. I will strengthen you, yes, I will help you, I will uphold you with My righteous right hand."

2. **Build your faith:** Faith grows through hearing and applying God's Word as shared in Romans 10:17. Surround yourself with testimonies of God's faithfulness to inspire your belief. A story published by Christian Broadcasting Network (*A Healing Confession*, 2013), tells of a woman who declared healing scriptures over her terminally ill husband for months. Despite the bleak medical prognosis, her unwavering faith and declarations brought about his complete recovery.

3. **Take action:** James 2:26: "Faith without works is dead". Demonstrate your belief by acting in alignment with your declarations. If you declare a financial breakthrough, start stewarding your resources wisely. If you declare healing, take steps toward health, such as eating well or seeking medical care while trusting God.

4. **Practice gratitude:** Gratitude shifts your focus from doubt to God's provision. Thank Him for past victories and answered prayers, which strengthens your faith for current declarations. A practical example of this can be found in the story of a missionary family who declared provision over their ministry despite limited funds (Ashcraft, 2019). By giving

thanks and trusting God, they witnessed miraculous financial support that exceeded their needs.

When you overcome doubt, your declaration becomes more powerful and effective. You can speak with boldness, knowing that God's promises are reliable. Additionally, conquering unbelief deepens your relationship with God, as it builds trust and dependence on Him.

George Muller, a 19th-century Christian evangelist and founder of orphanages, trusted God's provision without asking for money. He declared God's promises of provision daily and saw food, clothing, and financial resources arrive just in time for his children. Muller's story illustrates the power of unwavering faith in prophetic declarations (Stevens, 2017).

Faith in Prophetic Declarations

A compelling example of the power of faith-filled prophetic declarations is the testimony of a believer who, during a challenging time, received profound insights into their family's future. While visiting a family member in the hospital, they felt led to proclaim specific prophetic decrees over their family, trusting that these declarations would manifest in the coming year.

In a live broadcast, they shared these prophetic declarations, expressing unwavering faith in God's promises for their family's salvation and restoration. They emphasized the significance of speaking life and destiny over their loved ones, believing that their words, aligned with God's will, would bring about transformation (Living Faith Church Worldwide, 2023).

This testimony illustrates the impact of aligning one's heart and mind with God's Word and boldly declaring His promises. It serves as an encouragement to believers to speak life into their situations, trusting that God's purpose will be fulfilled in their lives through faith and prophetic declarations.

As we reflect on the impact of the spoken word, it becomes clear that God has gifted us with an incredible tool to shape our lives and align with His divine purposes. The examples from Scripture and real-life testimonies remind us that our declarations when grounded in faith, carry the power to break chains, open doors, and bring God's promises into reality. Yet, the effectiveness of these declarations hinges on more than just speaking; it requires intentionality, wisdom, and alignment with God's Word.

This leads us to a pivotal question: How can we craft declarations that are powerful and purposeful? What steps can we take to ensure our words reflect God's will and carry the authority He has entrusted to us?

In the next chapter, we will delve into crafting effective prophetic decrees. Here, we'll explore practical strategies to align your decrees with biblical principles, ensuring they are precise, faith-filled, and tailored to your unique circumstances. Together, we'll learn how to harness the full potential of this God-given tool, stepping boldly into the promises He has for you.

Chapter 3:

Crafting Effective Prophetic

Decrees

For by our words, you will be justified, and by your words, you will be condemned.
–Matthew 12:37

Words carry extraordinary weight. The words we choose to speak shape our reality, reflect the condition of our hearts, and influence the spiritual atmosphere around us. While this truth is awe-inspiring, it also carries great responsibility. Crafting prophetic decrees is more than simply speaking into the air. It is a deliberate, faith-filled process that requires understanding, alignment with God's will, and intentional action.

Let us begin by exploring the essential components of a prophetic decree. Each element plays a critical role in ensuring your word reflects God's will and carries His power. Through practical examples, biblical principles, and actionable steps, this chapter will equip you to step boldly into your spiritual authority with wisdom and confidence.

Components of a Powerful Decree

To be able to craft a powerful decree, the key lies in the truths that are anchored in Scripture and aligned with God's will. A well-crafted decree, one where we combine faith with action to bring spiritual realities into the physical realm, can be used as a tool to partner with God's purpose, calling His promises into existence. This section will delve deeper into two crucial components of effective decrees: Aligning your words with Scripture and ensuring they reflect God's will.

The components of a powerful decree act as a spiritual framework that ensures your declarations are impactful and grounded in God's truth. Without these foundational elements, a decree risks becoming empty words rather than faith-filled declarations. For example, anchoring a decree in Scripture ensures that it is based on God's unchanging promises rather than fleeting emotions or personal desires. This connection to the Word provides the decree with authority and divine backing, distinguishing it from mere positive affirmations.

Another key component is alignment with God's will, which ensures that the decree is in harmony with His greater plan for your life. This requires humility and discernment, recognizing that God's wisdom often exceeds human understanding. When you align your words with His will, you open the door for Him to work in ways that are transformative and eternal. Instead of decreeing wealth or material success, aligning with God's will might lead you to decree provision and stewardship, trusting Him to meet your needs in His perfect timing.

Faith is the activating force behind a powerful decree. Speaking words of faith changes the way you say them, with conviction and trust in God's power. A decree spoken without faith lacks the substance to bring about change. Mark 11:23 reminds us of this principle. Here, Jesus teaches us that faith-filled words spoken in alignment with God's will have the power to move obstacles and manifest His promises.

Lastly, consistency is an often overlooked component of effective decrees. A one-time declaration may inspire hope, but repeated, intentional decrees build spiritual momentum. The act of consistently speaking God's promises reinforces your faith, renews your mind, and invites His presence into your circumstances. It is through a persistent declaration that the truths of heaven are established on earth. As Isaiah 55:11 says, "So shall My word be that goes forth from My mouth; it shall not return to Me void, but it shall accomplish what I please, and it shall prosper in the thing for which I sent it." This verse assures us that God's Word, when spoken with faith and consistency, achieves His divine purpose.

Aligning Your Decree With Scripture

Scripture is the infallible Word of God, carrying His authority and power. When your decrees are rooted in the Bible, they carry a spiritual weight that extends beyond mere human speech. As 2 Timothy 3:16 affirms, "All Scripture is given by inspiration of God, and is profitable for doctrine, for reproof, for correction, for instruction in righteousness." This verse reminds us that God's Word provides guidance and power to craft a declaration that aligns with His nature and purposes.

Aligning decrees with Scripture ensures that we are not declaring words born out of our emotions, fears, or human desires but words that carry the authority of heaven. For instance, when faced with uncertainty, declaring Jeremiah 29:11 "For I know the thoughts that I think towards you, says the Lord, thoughts of peace and not of evil, to give you a future and a hope," anchors your hope in God's unchanging plans for your life.

Ezekiel and the Valley of Dry Bones

One powerful illustration of aligning decrees with Scripture is found in Ezekiel 37:1–10. God instructed the prophet Ezekiel to prophesy over a valley of dry bones, declaring that they would come to life. Ezekiel's declarations were not born of his imagination but spoken in obedience to God's command. As he prophesied, the bones came together, and life was restored. This story highlights the transformational power of speaking what God has already decreed.

Here are some practical steps to align with Scripture:

1. **Identify the promise:** Search the Bible for verses that speak directly to your situation. For example, if you need healing,

meditate on Isaiah 53:5, which states, "By His stripes we are healed,"

2. **Meditate on the Word:** Reflect on the Scripture to ensure that it resonates deeply within your heart.

3. **Personalize your decree:** Combine the Scripture with your own words to create a powerful and personal declaration.

Let's revisit the testimony of George Muller, the 19th-century English Christian evangelist we spoke about earlier. Muller relied solely on prayer and God's promises in Scripture to meet the needs of the children, (Stevens, 2017). On one occasion, with no food in the orphanage, Muller prayed and declared Psalm 37:25 "I have been young, and now am old; yet I have not seen the righteous forsaken, nor his descendants begging bread."

Shortly after, a baker arrived with fresh bread, followed by a milkman whose cart had broken down, providing enough for everyone. Muller's faith-filled decrees, rooted in Scripture, consistently brought divine provision.

Ensuring Your Declarations Are in Line With God's Will

Prophetic decrees don't just manipulate circumstances to fit our desires. They also form tools to align our lives with God's perfect will. As 1 John 5:14 assures us, "Now this is the confidence that we have in Him, that if we ask anything according to His will, He hears us."

When our declarations align with God's will, they carry His divine authority and power to bring about His purposes.

Jesus provides the ultimate example of submission to God's will in Matthew 26:39: "He went a little farther and fell on His face, and prayed, saying, 'O My Father, if it is possible, let this cup pass from Me; nevertheless, not as I will, but as You will." This moment highlights the balance between expressing our desires and yielding to God's greater plan. When we align our decrees with His will, we demonstrate trust in His wisdom and love.

Here are some practical strategies to align with God's will:

1. **Seek guidance in prayer:** Before making a decree, spend time in prayer to discern God's will for the situation.

2. **Consult Scripture:** Confirm that your declarations align with biblical principles and promises.

3. **Surrender your agenda:** Be willing to let go of personal preferences that may conflict with God's plan.

A contemporary example of aligning declarations with God's will can be found in the story of Corrie ten Boom, a Dutch Christian who helped hide Jews during World War II. After being imprisoned in a concentration camp, Corrie and her sister Betsie began declaring forgiveness and hope, despite their dire circumstances. They would pray and declare Scriptures like Romans 8:28, "And we know that all things work together for good to those who love God, to those who are the called according to His purpose." Their faith and alignment with God's will brought peace and even led to a spiritual revival among fellow prisoners.

The following are some benefits of alignment:

- **Clarity and confidence:** When your decrees align with God's Word and will, you can speak them with boldness and confidence. You know that you are partnering with Heaven to see His purpose fulfilled. This clarity also guards against frustration or disappointments, as you trust in His perfect timing and ways.

- **Spiritual power and impact:** Aligned decrees carry spiritual authority, opening doors for miracles and breakthroughs. Take Nehemiah 2:17–20 for example: When Nehemiah declared his intention to rebuild Jerusalem's walls, his alignment with God's will empowered him to overcome opposition and complete the task.

- **Transformational results:** When spoken with faith, aligned decrees can transform circumstances, bringing healing, provision, and restoration. They also deepen your relationship with God, as you witness His faithfulness in responding to His Word.

Aligning your decrees with Scripture and God's will is foundational for crafting declarations that are powerful and effective. These practices ensure that your words are not just expressions but vehicles for divine truth and authority. Whether you are declaring healing, peace, or provision, anchoring your words to the Bible and submitting to God's will guarantees that they will accomplish their purpose.

Examples of Prophetic Decrees

Prophetic decrees are targeted, faith-filled statements based on Scripture that invite God's intervention into specific areas of life. These decrees are acts of faith that align our words with God's promises. They empower us to declare God's truth over our circumstances. Let's explore examples of specific decrees for different areas of life, supported by biblical references and real-life applications.

Decrees for Healing

Healing is a promise deeply embedded in Scripture; Exodus 15:26 declares, "...For I am the Lord who heals you." Similarly, Isaiah 53:5 declares, "And by His stripes we are healed." These verses establish the foundation for decrees of healing, reminding us that Christ's sacrifice includes physical, emotional, and spiritual restoration. The following are some examples of healing decrees:

- **Decree over illness:** In the name of Jesus, I decree that my body is healed and whole. I declare that sickness has no authority over me because Jesus bore my infirmities and carried my diseases. By His stripes, I am healed (from Isaiah 53:5).

- **Decree over emotional wounds:** I decree that the peace of God, which surpasses all understanding, guards my heart and mind in Christ Jesus (in Philippians 4:7). I declare that I am not defined by past wounds but by God's truth and love.

The story of Dodie Osteen, the mother of Pastor Joel Osteen, is a powerful testimony of the healing power of decrees. Diagnosed with terminal liver cancer in the early 1980s, Dodie began speaking healing Scriptures daily. She declared verses like Psalm 107:20, "He sent His word and healed them, and delivered them from their destructions." Dodie's faith-filled decrees, combined with prayer, resulted in her complete healing, a testimony she continues to share today (Osteen, 2023).

Decrees for Financial Provision

The Bible is replete with promises of God's provision. Proverbs 10:22 reminds us, "The blessing of the Lord makes one rich, and He adds no sorrow with it." These truths empower us to declare financial abundance and provisions in alignment with God's principles.

- **Decree over scarcity:** I decree that I live in abundance because my God supplies all my needs according to His riches in glory by Christ Jesus (Philippians 4:19). I declare that poverty and scarcity have no place in my life, for the Lord is my shepherd, and I shall not want (Psalm 23:1).

- **Decree over financial wisdom:** I decree that I am a wise steward of God's resources. I declare that I make sound financial decisions guided by His Word and the Holy Spirit (Proverbs 3:5–6).

The testimony of David Green, the founder of Hobby Lobby, illustrates the power of faith and obedience in financial provision. Facing financial challenges in the company's early years, Green relied on biblical principles of generosity and stewardship (Green, 2017). By tithing and declaring God's promises over his business, he witnessed exponential growth, turning Hobby Lobby into a billion-dollar enterprise. Green often cites Malachi 3:10, which promises blessings for those who faithfully give to God.

Decrees of Protection

God's Word assures us of His divine protection. Psalm 91:11 declares, "For He shall give His angels charge over you, to keep you in all your ways." Similarly, Isaiah 54:17 reminds us, "No weapons formed against you shall prosper." These verses inspired decrees of safety and protection in times of danger or uncertainty.

- **Decree over family:** I decree that no harm shall befall my family. The Lord is our refuge and fortress, and we dwell under the shadow of His wings (Psalm 91:1–2). No weapon formed against us shall prosper, and every tongue that rises against us in judgment shall be condemned (Isaiah 45:17).

- **Decree over travel:** I decree that the Lord guards my going out and coming in from this time forth and forevermore (Psalm 121:8). I declare that His angels encamp around me, protecting me from harm.

One inspiring story of God's protection involves missionary John G. Paton. While serving in the New Hebrides Islands, hostile natives surrounded his home, intent on burning it down. Paton and his wife prayed fervently, declaring God's protection. Miraculously, the attackers retreated without explanation. Later, a tribal chief confessed that they had seen a host of men in shining garments guarding the house, a divine intervention that fulfilled Psalm 34:7: "The angel of the Lord encamps all around those who fear Him, and delivers them."

Decrees for Emotional and Mental Peace

In a world often plagued by anxiety and fear. God offers peace as a promise. John 14:27 says, "Peace I leave with you, My peace I give to you; not as the world gives do I give to you. Let not our heart be troubled, neither let it be afraid." Philippians 4:6–7 urges believers to replace worry with prayer, promising peace that surpasses understanding.

- **Decree over anxiety:** I decree that I am free from anxiety and fear. The peace of God guards my heart and mind in Christ Jesus, and I cast all my cares on Him because He cares for me (Philippians 4:6–7; 1 Peter 5:7).

- **Decree over restlessness:** I decree that my soul finds rest in God alone. I declare that His presence brings fullness of joy and perfect peace (Psalm 62:1; Psalm 16:11).

Joyce Meyer, a well-known Christian author and speaker, has shared her struggles with anxiety and fear. Through prayer and declarations of Scripture, she overcame these challenges. One verse she frequently declared was Isaiah 26:3: "You will keep him in perfect peace, whose mind is stayed on You because he trusts in You." Her testimony demonstrates how declaring God's promises can bring freedom from mental struggles.

Decrees for Spiritual Growth and Purpose

God desires for His children to grow spiritually and fulfill their divine purpose. Jeremiah 29:11 affirms that His plans are for our welfare and not for evil, to give us a future and hope. Philippians 1:6 says, "He who has begun a good work in you will complete it until the day of Jesus Christ."

- **Decree for growth:** I decree that I am growing daily in the knowledge of God's Word. I declare that I am being transformed into the image of Christ (2 Corinthians 3:18).

- **Decree over purpose:** I decree that I walk in the plans and purposes God has for me. I declare that I am equipped for every good work and fulfill the calling He has placed on my life (Ephesians 2:10).

Billy Graham, one of the most influential evangelists of all time, often prayed and declared Scriptures over his ministry. His commitment to aligning his life with God's Word and decreeing purpose-filled promises enabled him to reach millions with the gospel. Graham's example highlights the power of prophetic decrees in fulfilling divine destiny.

Examples of prophetic decree explored in this chapter reveal the transformative power of aligning our words with God's truth. Whether we seek healing, financial provision, protection, peace, or spiritual growth, decrees give us a way to partner with heaven, releasing the authority of God's promises into our lives. Each declaration is a step of faith, a proclamation that shifts our focus from the problem to the solution, from our limitations to God's limitless power.

However, to decree effectively, we must first understand the foundation of our declarations of God's promises. These promises are eternal truths spoken by the One who cannot lie. In the next chapter, we will dive deeper into what it means to decree God's promises. You'll learn how to identify His promises in Scripture, apply them to your circumstances, and speak them with unwavering faith.

Chapter 4:

Decreeing God's Promises

For all the promises of God in Him are "Yes," and in Him "Amen,"
to the glory of God through us. –2 Corinthians 1:20

God's promises are a testament to His unchanging character and boundless love for His children. They are the inheritance of every believer, offered through the covenant relationship we have in Christ. Yet, promises do not manifest automatically in our lives. Like a treasure that must be discovered, claimed, and enjoyed, God's promises require us to take active steps of faith to bring them into our realities. One of the most effective ways to do this is through prophetic decrees.

When we decree God's promises, we align ourselves with His Word and activate the spiritual principles that govern the kingdom of heaven. Speaking these promises aloud with faith and conviction is not a passive exercise but a declaration of partnership with God's will. This practice transforms situations, strengthens faith, and reinforces the truth of God's unchanging love.

In this chapter, we'll explore what it means to decree God's promises, why it is a vital practice for every believer, and how to stand firmly on these promises in the face of challenges. You will learn to identify His promises in Scripture and wield them as tools to overcome adversity, build confidence, and bring glory to His name.

Understanding God's Promises

At its core, a promise is a commitment—a declaration of intent. In human terms, promises can be fragile, often broken due to circumstances or human frailty. But God's promises are different. They are eternal, unchanging, and unbreakable because they flow from His perfect nature.

God's promises serve as the anchor for our faith. When the storms of life rage, they remind us of His faithfulness. In the Bible, His promises are vast and cover every area of human need. From peace in troubled times to health for the sick, provision in scarcity, and victory over trials, these assurances provide hope and direction.

God's Word and His promises matter because they reflect His covenant relationship with us. They reveal His heart and intentions, inviting us to trust and rest in His plans. When we understand these promises, we gain a deeper appreciation of His love and also empower ourselves to live victoriously, regardless of life's challenges.

God's promises are divine assurances spoken by an unchanging God who is faithful to His Word. The Bible says in Numbers 23:19, "God is not a man, that He should lie, nor a son of man, that He should repent. Has He said, and will He not do? Or has He spoken, and will

He not make it good?" These words remind us that God's promises are trustworthy and dependable.

When we identify and stand on God's promises, we anchor our faith to His truth, allowing us to rise above life's uncertainties. But how do we recognize these promises, and what does it mean to stand on them? This is a personal journey that includes knowing His Word, personalizing His truths, and holding onto them with unshakable faith.

Identifying and Standing on the Promises of God

The Bible is filled with thousands of promises, covering every conceivable aspect of life. From spiritual salvation to physical healing, provision, and protection, God's promises are as vast and varied as the needs of humanity. However, to identify these promises, we must engage with Scripture intentionally and prayerfully.

1. **Read the Bible with purpose:** When reading Scripture, approach it with a heart seeking God's direction. As you study, look for verses that resonate with your current situation or need. Here are some examples:

   a. If you are struggling with fear, meditate on 2 Timothy 1:7: "For God has not given us a spirit of fear, but of power and of love and of a sound mind."

   b. For provision, turn to Philippians 4:19: "And my God shall supply all your need according to His riches in glory by Christ Jesus."

   c. For peace during struggles, reflect on Isaiah 26:3: "You will keep him in perfect peace, whose mind is stayed on You, because he trusts in You."

   d. For healing, rely on Isaiah 53:5: "But He was wounded for our transgressions, He was bruised for our iniquities; the chastisement for our peace was upon Him, and by His stripes we are healed."

   e. If you are seeking wisdom, ponder upon James 1:5: "If any of you lacks wisdom, let him ask of God, who gives to all liberally and without reproach, and it will be given to him."

2. **Use a concordance or study tool:** A concordance or Bible study tool can help you locate promises relevant to your needs. These resources group Scriptures by topic, making it

easier to find verses on healing, finances, relationships, or peace.

3. **Pray for revelations:** Ask the Holy Spirit to reveal promises specific to your situations. Jesus said in John 16:13, "However, when He, the Spirit of truth, has come, He will guide you into all truth." Trust the Spirit to guide your understanding as you seek God's promises.

Personalizing God's Promises

Once you've identified a promise, the next step is to personalize it. This means taking the general truth of Scripture and making it specific to your life. Personalizing Scripture transforms it from a universal truth into a deeply personal declaration. Examples:

- Psalm 23:1 says, "The Lord is my shepherd; I shall not want." You can use this to declare: *The Lord is my Shepard. I lack nothing in my life because He provides for all my needs.*

- Instead of decreeing, "You will keep him in perfect peace," declare, *God will keep me, [your name] in perfect peace because I trust in Him.*

Personalization isn't just about changing the words; it's about internalizing God's promise and letting it take root in your heart. By doing so, you make the promise a central part of your faith journey.

What It Means to Stand on God's Promises

Standing on God's promises means holding onto His Word with unwavering faith, even when circumstances challenge your belief. It's about choosing to trust what God says over what you see, hear, or feel.

- **Holding fast in difficult times:** Life often presents situations that test our faith. Imagine facing a serious illness and holding onto Isaiah 53:5: "By His stripes, we are healed." It's easy to question this promise when symptoms persist, but standing on God's Word means choosing to believe in His healing power, even when the manifestation isn't immediate. Consider the story of Hannah in 1 Samuel. She desperately desired a child and endured years of barrenness and ridicule. Yet, she stood on her faith in God's ability to fulfill His promise. Eventually, her steadfast trust was rewarded, and she gave birth to Samuel, a prophet who would impact Israel's history.

- **Declaring the promise aloud:** Speaking God's promises is an act of faith and spiritual warfare. It aligns your words with God's truth, countering the enemy's lies and reinforcing your belief. For example, if you're battling fear, declaring Psalm 27:1, "The Lord is my light and my salvation; whom shall I fear?" reminds you of God's protection and loosens fear's hold.

- **Taking action in faith:** Faith without works is dead as found in James 2:17. Standing on a promise often requires action. If you believe in financial provision, align your actions with your faith by being a good steward of your resources, giving generously and trusting God's guidance.

Overcoming Doubt While Standing on Promises

Doubt is a natural human response, especially when waiting for promises to manifest. To overcome doubt, you need to actively choose faith and reinforce God's truth in your life.

1. **Meditate on God's faithfulness:** Reflect on past instances where God has come through for you. Recalling His

faithfulness builds confidence in His ability to fulfill His promises again.

2. **Surround yourself with encouragement:** Join a community of believers who can pray with you, share testimonies, and encourage you to persevere.

3. **Replace doubt with the Word:** Every time a doubtful thought arises, counter it with Scripture. When Abraham doubted God's promise of a son, he didn't dwell on his own limitations. Instead, he focused on God's ability, as Romans 4:21 describes: "And being fully convinced that what He had promised He was also able to perform."

A modern testimony of standing on God's promises comes from a young woman diagnosed with an incurable disease. Doctors gave her little hope, but she clung to God's Word, particularly Isaiah 53:5, declaring it every day. She wrote the verse on sticky notes and placed them around her home, repeating it daily despite worsening symptoms.

Over time, her faith and declarations were rewarded. She experienced complete healing, astonishing her doctors. Her testimony reminds us of the power of standing on God's promises and trusting His for the impossible.

You may also try these practical strategies for standing on promises during challenging times:

1. **Anchor yourself in the Word:** Read, study, and memorize Scripture relevant to your needs.

2. **Create a promise journal:** Write down the promises you believe in and the corresponding Scripture references.

3. **Pray with expectation:** Speak God's promises in prayer, thanking Him in advance for their fulfillment.

4. **Practice gratitude:** Celebrate small victories as evidence of God's faithfulness.

God's promises are unshakable truths designed to guide and sustain us. When you identify and stand on these promises, you position yourself to receive His blessings and bring glory to His name. As you hold onto His promises, trust that His timing and plans are perfect, and His Word never fails.

How to Activate Promises Through Decrees

God's promises are eternal truths, but they are not meant to remain dormant or untapped. To experience their full power, we must activate them through faith-filled declarations, also known as decrees. When we decree God's promises, we align our words with His Word, creating a spiritual agreement that releases His will into our lives. As

Proverbs 18:21 reminds us, "Death and life are in the power of the tongue, and those who love it will eat its fruit." Through decrees, we can actively partake in the fruit of God's promises.

Activation is the step through which we move from belief to action. It's the spiritual equivalent of flipping a switch to turn on a light. The promises of God are always available, but decreeing them invites His power to flow into your specific situation. When you speak God's Word with faith, you unleash spiritual forces that bring transformation.

Consider the account of creation in Genesis. God spoke the world into existence in Genesis 1:3: "Then God said, 'Let there be light', and there was light." His words were the mechanism of creation. Similarly, when we decree His promises, we invite divine action into our lives.

Practical Steps to Decree God's Promises Over Your Life

1. **Know the promise you're decreeing:** Before you can decree a promise, you must identify it. Search Scripture for verses that address your specific need, such as healing, provision, or peace. Understanding the context and meaning of the verse is

essential to ensure your declaration aligns with God's will. Example:

   a. For healing, declare Isaiah 53:5, speaking your name and health issue as healed.

   b. For provision, use Philippians 4:19, declaring your needs are met while using this verse.

2. **Speak with faith and conviction:** Decrees are not mere recitations; they are faith-filled proclamations. Speak with the assurance that God's Word is true and His promises are sure. Hebrews 11:1 reminds us, "Now faith is the substance of things hoped for, the evidence of things not seen." When you decree, envision the promise already fulfilled. Take, for example, this declaration for healing:

a. In the name of Jesus, I declare that by His stripes, I am healed. I rebuke sickness and stand in agreement with God's promise of wholeness and restoration in my body.

3. **Combine declarations with prayer:** Prayer and decrees go hand in hand. While decrees affirm God's promises, prayer allows for intimate communication with Him. When you decree, follow it with thanksgiving and petition. For example, if you're decreeing financial provision, pray the following:

   a. Lord, I thank You for being Jehovah-Jireh, my provider. I trust in Your Word that You will supply all my needs. I decree abundance and provision in every area of my life according to Philippians 4:19.

4. **Anchor decrees in Scripture:** Ensure your decrees are firmly rooted in God's Word. Declarations based on biblical truths carry divine authority and cannot be shaken. This prevents you from making decrees that stem from personal desires rather than God's will. Here's an example of peace:

   a. Decree: I declare peace over my life and my household.

   b. Anchor verse: "Peace I leave with you, My peace I give to you; not as the world gives do I give to you. Let not your heart be troubled, neither let it be afraid" (Johan 14:27).

5. **Decree regularly and persistently:** Activation often requires consistency. The Bible emphasizes persistence, as seen in the parable of the persistent window in Luke 18:1–8. Keep decreeing God's promises, even if the manifestation

isn't immediate. This builds your faith and keeps your focus on His Word. Here's an example of a decree you can make daily if you believe in a breakthrough:

    a. I declare that the God of breakthroughs is working in my life. No weapon formed against me shall prosper, and I will walk in victory according to His promises.

6. **Guard your words against negativity:** Faith-filled decrees can be nullified by negative or contradictory words. Be vigilant about what you speak about yourself and your circumstances. James 3:10 warns, "Out of the same mouth proceed blessing and cursing. My brethren, these things ought not to be so." Choose to speak life and align your words with God's truth.

7. **Involve others in agreement:** There is power in corporate prayer and agreement. Jesus said in Matthew 18:19, "Again I say to you that if two of you agree on earth concerning anything that they ask, it will be done for them by My Father in heaven." Share your decrees with trusted believers who can stand in agreement with you. Example:

    a. If you're decreeing restoration in your family, ask a friend or pastor to join you in declaring unity and healing.

8. **Celebrate small victories:** As you begin to see God's promises unfold, celebrate every step of progress. Gratitude

reinforces your faith and keeps you focused on His goodness. Here's an example:

    a. If you've been decreeing healing and noticed even minor improvements, thank God for the work He's doing.

Biblical Examples of Activating Promises Through Decrees

Joshua's declaration of victory over Jericho is an extraordinary example of faith and obedience in action. God had already promised Joshua that Jericho would be delivered into his hands, yet the fulfillment of that promise required specific actions and a spoken proclamation. As recorded in Joshua 6:20, "So the people shouted when the priests blew the trumpets. And it happened when the people heard the sound of the trumpet, and the people shouted with a great shout, that the wall fell down flat. Then the people went up into the city, every man straight before him, and they took the city."

Joshua's shout was not merely a loud noise; it was an act of faith, a decree rooted in the assurance of God's promise. The Israelites' obedience to march around the city for seven days and shout at the appointed time demonstrated the relationship between action, decree, and faith. Their victory was not achieved by their strength but by aligning their words and actions with God's specific instructions. This story reminds us that speaking God's promises with faith can bring down seemingly insurmountable obstacles in our lives.

Elijah's story in 1 Kings 18:41–45 provides another striking example of activating promises through decrees. After a three-and-a-half-year drought, Elijah declared to King Ahab, "Go up, eat and drink; for there is the sound of abundance of rain." At this point, no visible sign of rain existed, yet Elijah spoke as if the promise had already manifested.

Elijah's declaration was followed by persistent action, he climbed to the top of Mount Carmel and prayed fervently. Despite sending his servant seven times to check for signs of rain, Elijah did not waver. On the seventh time, the servant reported a small cloud rising from the sea, and soon after, the heavens opened. Elijah's unwavering faith and bold decree aligned with God's Word, leading to the fulfillment of His promise. This example illustrates the new power of persistence in decreeing and the necessity of faith even when immediate evidence is absent.

Real-Life Testimony of Provision Through Decrees

In modern times, the power of decreeing God's promises remains just as relevant. One inspiring testimony is that of a single mother going through a phase of financial hardship. With bills piling up and no clear way forward, she turned to Scripture and began decreeing Philippians 4:19 over her situation. Each morning, she spoke these words aloud: *I decree that God is my provider. He will meet every financial need in my household. I trust in His riches, not my circumstances.*

Her declarations were more than recitations; they were expressions of faith and a way of aligning her heart and mind with God's promises. Over time, remarkable changes unfolded. She received an unexpected promotion at work, friends offered unsolicited financial assistance, and several of her monthly expenses were reduced or eliminated entirely.

This testimony highlights a crucial truth. Decreeing on God's promises is not a magic formula but a way to focus your faith and expectations on His provision. When we speak His Word with belief, it shapes our perspective, opens doors for divine intervention, and allows us to witness His promises fulfilled.

These examples, whether from Scripture or real life, reveal consistent themes. First, decrees must be rooted in God's promises, not in human desire or fleeting emotions. Second, faith is the foundation that activates the power of a decree. Third, persistence in prayer and declaration is vital, as God often works through processes that require patience and trust.

As we have seen, decreeing God's promises activates His Word in our lives, bringing His truth to bear on our circumstances. These declarations align us with His will, strengthen our faith, and release His blessings. Yet, the power of decrees goes beyond claiming promises for provision, healing, or guidance, extending into spiritual warfare.

In a world where believers face unseen battles, decrees become weapons of authority to confront and dismantle spiritual strongholds. These strongholds, whether manifesting as fear, addiction, generational patterns, or deeply ingrained lies, can be broken through a faith-filled declaration that proclaims God's victory.

In the next chapter, we will explore how decrees can be used to confront and break spiritual strongholds. We'll uncover the biblical foundation for this practice, examine real-life examples, and provide practical strategies to walk in the freedom and authority Christ has given us. As you turn the page, prepare to learn how your words, empowered by Scripture, can tear down barriers and establish God's truth in every area of your life.

Chapter 5:

Breaking Strongholds

With Decrees

For the weapons of our warfare are not carnal but mighty in God for pulling down strongholds. –2 Corinthians 10:4

The concept of breaking strongholds is vital for spiritual freedom. A stronghold is any thought pattern, belief system, or habit that opposes God's truth and holds us captive. These strongholds can manifest as fear, doubt, addiction, unforgiveness, or other barriers that hinder spiritual growth and the fulfillment of God's promises in our lives.

The power of prophetic decrees lies in their ability to dismantle these fortresses. When you speak God's Word over your life, it penetrates spiritual resistance, aligning your heart and mind with His will. This chapter will explore how decrees can become an effective tool for identifying, addressing, and demolishing strongholds.

David's confrontation with Goliath illustrates the power of declaring God's authority over strongholds. Goliath was not just a physical giant but a symbol of intimidation and fear. Before David even swung on his sling, he boldly declared in 1 Samuel 17:45, "You come to me with a sword, with a spear, and with a javelin. But I come to you in the name of the Lord of hosts, the God of the armies of Israel, whom you have defied."

David's words were not idle; they were rooted in his faith in God's power. This declaration broke the stronghold of fear that paralyzed Israel's army and set the stage for victory. David's decree showed that speaking God's truth can dismantle even the most intimidating strongholds.

A real-life example involves a man named Joe Turner, who struggled with drug addiction. After years of failed attempts to quit on his own, he turned to his faith for strength. Joe began to proclaim Scriptures daily, such as Philippians 4:13: "I can do all things through Christ who strengthens me."

Each morning, he declared: "I decree that addiction has no power over me. In Jesus' name, I am free, and His strength is made perfect in my weakness." Over time, these decrees, paired with prayer and accountability, reshaped his mindset. What once felt impossible became achievable as he experienced freedom through God's strength. His consistent declarations helped him break the chains of addiction and step into a life of victory (Frederickson, 2015).

Strongholds keep us from living in the fullness of God's promises. They distort our view of His truth, limit our faith, and prevent us from fulfilling His purpose. By identifying and addressing these areas, we open ourselves to spiritual breakthroughs and deeper intimacy with God.

Identifying Spiritual Strongholds

Spiritual strongholds are barriers that hinder your spiritual growth, distort your identity in Christ, and block the fulfillment of God's promises. These are not merely emotional or psychological struggles; they are deeply rooted patterns of thoughts, belief systems, or behaviors that stand in opposition to God's truth.

The first step to breaking free from the grips of strongholds is the ability to understand and identify each stronghold. When you recognize what they are and how they operate, you can effectively confront and dismantle them using God's Word.

Strongholds often take root in areas where we feel most vulnerable or have experienced repeated challenges. Below are some of the most common areas where spiritual strongholds can develop, along with biblical insights and real-life testimonies that show how God's power can bring deliverance.

Fear and Anxiety

Fear is one of the most common strongholds. It can manifest as worry, doubt, or a paralyzing inability to move forward. This stronghold feeds on lies and distorts your view of God's protection and provision. The Bible repeatedly assures us of God's presence and power over fear. In Isaiah 41:10, God declares, "Fear not, for I am with you; be not dismayed, for I am your God. I will strengthen you. Yes, I will help you, I will uphold you with My righteous right hand."

A woman named Sarah shared her testimony on CBN News about struggling with overwhelming fear after a traumatic car accident (CBN Europe, 2022). Her fear of driving became a crippling stronghold. After months of avoiding the road, she turned to God's Word, declaring 2 Timothy 1:7: "For God has not given us a spirit of fear, but of power and of love and of a sound mind."

Sarah began speaking the truth daily, praying for courage. Slowly, she felt her fear lose its hold. One day, she got behind the wheel again, realizing that God's promises had empowered her to overcome what once seemed insurmountable.

Poverty and Scarcity

Another stronghold is rooted in the belief that you will never have enough. This mindset creates a cycle of worry and holds you back from trusting God as your provider. The Bible makes it clear that poverty is not God's plan for His children. Philippians 4:19 states, "And my God shall supply all your need according to His riches in glory by Christ Jesus." God desires to bless His people so they can live in freedom and generosity.

Jason, a struggling business owner, shared his story on Christian Broadcasting Network (VertexValue, 2024). He felt trapped in a financial stronghold, consistently worrying about how he would pay his bills. After hearing a sermon on God's provision, Jason began declaring verses like Psalm 23:1: "The Lord is my shepherd; I shall not want."

Over time, his perspective shifted. Jason took bold steps in faith, such as tithing and giving, even during tight months. Miraculously, his business started to grow and unexpected contracts began to flow in. His testimony shows that aligning your mindset with God's truth can break the stronghold of poverty.

Sickness and Disease

Sickness can become a stronghold when it leads to despair, hopelessness, or doubt in God's ability to heal. While physical illness is a reality of living in a fallen world, the Bible provides countless examples of God's healing power. Isaiah 53:5 reminds us, "But He was wounded for our transgressions, He was bruised for our iniquities; the chastisement for our peace was upon Him, and by His stripes, we are healed." Believing in God's healing promises can help you resist the stronghold of sickness and embrace faith for recovery.

Daniel Biwila (2021) shared his testimony in The Christian Science Journal about suffering from chronic migraines that significantly impacted his daily life. By studying the Bible and embracing spiritual truths, he found relief. Daniel reflected on Jeremiah 30:17: "For I will restore health unto thee, and I will heal thee of thy wounds, saith the Lord."

When he aligned his thoughts with this promise, he experienced a complete cessation of migraines, attributing his healing to a deeper understanding of God's care and the transformative power of spiritual thinking. This shared testimony provides us with the profound impact of embracing God's promises and the potential for healing through faith and spiritual alignment.

Unforgiveness and Bitterness

Unforgiveness is a stronghold that binds you to the past and prevents spiritual growth. Holding on to grudges or resentment gives the enemy a foothold in your life. Jesus taught the importance of forgiveness in Matthew 6:14-15: "For if you forgive men their trespasses, your heavenly Father will also forgive you. But if you do not forgive men their trespasses, neither will your Father forgive your trespasses." Releasing others through forgiveness allows God's peace to flow freely in your life.

Linda's story shared on Desiring God, demonstrates the power of forgiveness (Gustafson, 2023). After being betrayed by a close friend, Linda carried bitterness for years. One day, during a church service, she heard a message in Ephesians 4:32: "And be kind to one another, tenderhearted, forgiving one another, even as God in Christ forgave you."

Convinced, she chose to forgive her friend. The act of speaking forgiveness aloud broke the chains of resentment, and Linda experienced a new level of freedom and joy in her relationship with God.

Negative Self-Image and Shame

A negative self-image is a stronghold that distorts your identity in Christ. Shame and feelings of inadequacy can cause you to doubt God's love and purpose for your life. The Bible counters this with the truth of your worth in God's eyes. Psalm 139:14 declares, "I will praise You, for I am fearfully and wonderfully made; Marvelous as Your works, and that my soul knows very well."

A young woman named Emily shared her story on IAmSecond.com (Bofelo, 2024). Struggling with self-esteem after years of rejection, Emily believed she was unlovable. Through counseling and meditating on verses like Romans 8:1: "There is therefore now no condemnation to those who are in Christ Jesus, who do not walk according to the flesh, but according to the Spirit." She began to see herself as God does. Emily's transformation came as she replaced the lies of shame with the truth of Scripture, reclaiming her identity as a beloved child of God.

Identifying spiritual strongholds is a crucial first step in overcoming them. When you recognize these areas in your life, you can begin addressing them with God's Word and power. No matter how deeply entrenched a stronghold may seem, remember that God's truth is mightier. Through faith, prayer, and His Word, you can experience freedom and victory in every area of your life.

Strategies for Breaking Strongholds

Strongholds are deeply entrenched patterns of thought or behavior that resist change and keep people bound in fear, sin, sickness, and scarcity. Breaking these spiritual barriers requires intentional effort and divine authority. One of the most effective strategies is employing prophetic decrees: speaking God's Word over the situation with authority and faith. Let's explore how to effectively use prophetic decrees to tear down strongholds with practical steps and biblical examples to encourage you to walk in freedom.

How to Use Prophetic Decrees to Tear Down Strongholds

Prophetic decrees are powerful because they align your words with God's truth, which has the power to dismantle lies and break chains. Proverbs 18:21 reminds us, "Death and life are in the power of the tongue..." The words you speak can either sustain a stronghold or destroy it. The key is to wield this weapon intentionally, with faith and in alignment with Scripture.

1. **Identify the stronghold and its root cause:** To effectively tear down a stronghold, you must first identify it. Is the stronghold a spirit of fear as mentioned in 2 Timothy 1:7: "For God has not given us a spirit of fear, but of power and of love and of a sound mind." Or perhaps it's a pattern of poverty, discouragement, or addiction. Spend time in prayer, asking God to reveal the lies you've believed or areas where the enemy has taken ground in your life.

   a. **Example:** Imagine a person struggling with self-doubt rooted in years of negative words spoken over them. Recognizing this as a stronghold is the first step in breaking free. Once you know the root, you can address it with specific declarations rooted in God's Word.

2. **Choose Scripture that counters the stronghold:** Prophetic decrees are most powerful when they're grounded in Scripture. The Bible contains specific promises and truths that

apply to every stronghold. When you speak these words, you are not just reciting Scripture; you are wielding it as a sword as described in Ephesians 6:17: "And take the helmet of salvation, and the sword of the Spirit, which is the Word of God."

a. **For fear:** Declare Isaiah 35:4: "Say to those who are fearful-hearted, 'Be strong, do not fear! Behold, your God will come with vengeance, with the recompense of God; He will come and save you," or Psalm 27:1: "The Lord is my light and my salvation; whom shall I fear? The Lord is the strength of my life; of whom shall I be afraid?"

b. **For poverty:** Declare Psalm 37:25, "I have been young, and now am old; yet I have not seen the righteous forsaken, nor his descendants begging bread," or try Deuteronomy 28:12: "The Lord will open to you His good treasure, the heavens, to give the rain to your land in its season, and to bless all the work of your hand. You shall lend to many nations, but you shall not borrow."

c. **For addiction:** Declare Romans 6:14: "For sin shall not have dominion over you, for you are not under law but under grace," or try Galatians 5:1: "Stand fast therefore in the liberty by which Christ has made us free, and do not be entangled again with a yoke of bondage."

d. **For sickness:** Declare Exodus 23:25: "So you shall serve the Lord your God, and He will bless your bread and your water. And I will take sickness away from the midst of you." Another example is Psalm 103:2-3: "Bless the Lord, O my soul, and forget not all His benefits: who forgives all your iniquities, who heals all your diseases."

e. **For anxiety and worry:** Declare Philippians 4:6–7: "Be anxious for nothing, but in everything by prayer and supplication, with thanksgiving, let our requests be made known to God; and the peace of God, which surpasses all understanding, will guard your hearts and minds through Christ Jesus." Another example is found in 1 Peter 5:7: "Casting all your care upon Him, for He cares for you."

f. **For depression or hopelessness:** Declare Isaiah 61:3: "To console those who mourn in Zion, to give them beauty for ashes, the oil of joy for the morning, the garment of praise for the spirit of heaviness; that they may be called trees of righteousness, the planting of the Lord, that He may be glorified," or perhaps Psalm 42:11: "Why are you cast down, O my soul? And why are you disquieted within me? Hope in God; for I shall yet praise Him, the help of my countenance and my God."

g. **For broken relationships:** Declare Ephesians 4:31–32: "Let all bitterness, wrath, anger, clamor, and evil speaking be put away from you, with all malice. And be kind to one another, tenderhearted, forgiving one another, even as God in Christ forgave you." Also, declare Matthew 18:21–22: "Then Peter came to Him and said, 'Lord, how often shall my brother sin against me, and I forgive him? Up to seven times?' Jesus said to him, 'I do not say to you, up to seven times, but up to seventy times seven.'"

3. **Speak with authority and conviction:** When making prophetic decrees, it's important to speak with authority. As a believer, you have been given authority through Christ as stated in Luke 10:19: "Behold, I give you the authority to trample on serpents and scorpions, and over all the power of the enemy, and nothing shall by any means hurt you."

    a. **Practical example:** If you are battling sickness, don't just hope for healing, declare it with boldness. Declare Isaiah 53:5: "I decree that by His stripes, I am healed. Sickness has no place in my body. My body aligns with God's design for health and wholeness." Speaking with conviction reinforces your faith and disarms the enemy's lies.

4. **Engage in persistent decrees:** Breaking strongholds is often not a one-time event. Just as Joshua and the Israelites circled Jericho for seven days before the wall came down, as found in Joshua 6, you may need to repeatedly decree God's promises over your situation. Persistent declarations build faith and weaken the grip of the stronghold.

    a. **Biblical example:** Elijah's persistent prayer for rain after a drought in 1 Kings 18:41–45 teaches us the importance of resistance. Even when no evidence of change was visible, Elijah continued to pray and declare until the promise was fulfilled.

5. **Accompany decrees with obedience and action:** Prophetic decrees are powerful, but they must be accompanied by obedience to God's Word. James 2:17 reminds us, "Faith by itself if it does not have works, is dead." If you are decreeing financial provision, ask God to guide your financial decisions and take practical steps to steward your resources well.

   a. **Example:** A woman struggling with fear decreed Isaiah 41:10 daily. At the same time, she actively sought opportunities to step out in faith, such as speaking in public or trying new challenges. The combination of her declarations and actions led to freedom from fear.

6. **Use decrees in corporate prayer:** Strongholds can also affect families, communities, or nations. Engaging in corporate prayer and making decrees as a group can amplify their power. Matthew 18:19 says, "Again I say to you that if two of you agree on earth concerning anything that they ask, it will be done for them by My Father in heaven."

   a. **Real-life testimony:** In a small town in Kansas, a group of believers gathered weekly to pray against a spirit of division in their community. They declared unity and peace using Ephesians 4:3: "Endeavoring to keep the unity of the Spirit in the bond of peace." Over time, relationships between local churches were restored, and the community saw a revival of cooperation and love.

7. **Stand firm in faith and reject doubt:** Doubt undermines the power of your declaration. James 1:6 warns, "But let him ask in faith, with no doubting, for he who doubts is like a wave of the sea driven and tossed by the wind." Stand firm in the promises of God, even when circumstances seem unchanged.

   a. **Biblical example:** Abraham is a powerful example of unwavering faith. Romans 4:20–21 states, "He did not waver at the promise of God through unbelief, but was strengthened in faith, giving the glory of God, and being fully convinced that what He had promised He was also able to perform."

The Transformative Impact of Prophetic Decrees

Breaking strongholds through prophetic decrees is a partnership with God's divine power. It requires faith, persistence, and alignment with His Word. When you speak His promises with authority, you tap into the creative power that brings transformations.

Whatever stronghold you are facing, know that it is not permanent. The same God who brought down the walls of Jericho and set captives free is working on your behalf. Use the strategies outlined here to declare His truth over your life, and watch as His power breaks every chain.

2 Corinthians 10:4-5 says, "For the weapons of our warfare are not carnal but mighty in God for pulling down strongholds, casting down arguments and every high thing that exalts itself against the knowledge

of God, bringing every thought into captivity to the obedience of Christ."

As strongholds are torn down, a new chapter of spiritual growth and peace begins. However, breaking free from strongholds is not just about liberation; it is also about building a life fortified by God's presence and favor. Daily decrees play a vital role in maintaining this freedom, covering your life with divine protection and blessing.

In chapter 6, we will shift from warfare to daily living, exploring how proactive declarations can position you under the constant covering of God's love and provision. You'll discover how to decree His promises for safety, health, provision, and joy, creating an atmosphere of peace and victory in every area of life. Let's continue this journey of transformation and empowerment!

Chapter 6:

Daily Decrees for Divine

Protection and Blessing

The Lord shall preserve your going out and your coming in from this time forth, and even forevermore. –Psalm 121:8

Every day brings its own challenges and opportunities, and as believers, we are called to start each day rooted in God's promises. Daily decrees are more than words; they are spiritual alignment that invites divine protection, provision, and blessing into our lives.

Think of daily decrees as the spiritual armor you put on each morning. They set the tone for the day, reinforcing faith, guarding against doubt, and declaring the authority of God's Word over every situation. The Bible affirms this in Proverbs 18:21, "Death and life are in the power of the tongue, and those who live it will eat its fruit." By speaking life daily, you align your thoughts, emotions, and actions with God's purpose, shielding yourself from negativity and embracing His abundant promises.

This chapter will talk about the practice of creating a daily routine of declarations and provide practical strategies to integrate them into your life. You will learn how consistent, intentional decrees create a spiritual environment where divine protection and blessings can flow freely.

Daily Routine of Declarations

Developing a daily routine of speaking God's Word is much like planting seeds. Over time, these words of faith take root in our hearts and produce a harvest of peace, joy, and divine favor. While establishing this habit requires discipline and intentionality, the rewards are immeasurable. A life built on daily declarations is a life fortified by God's truth.

Each morning presents an opportunity to start fresh, to focus your mind and heart on God's promises before the demands of the day take over. Begin by declaring Scripture-based traits over your life. For example, Psalm 91:11 reminds us of God's protective care, "For He shall give His angels charge over you, to keep you in all your ways." Speaking this verse around establishes a spiritual covering, reinforcing the assurance that God's angels are actively working to safeguard you. By starting your day this way, you prepare your mind and spirit to face the day's challenges with confidence and peace.

Declarations are not limited to the morning; they are tools to use throughout the day. When faced with stress, fear, or uncertainty, turn to God's Word for reassurance. Philippians 4:13 declares, "I can do all things through Christ who strengthens me." Repeating this truth during difficult moments shifts your focus from the problem to God's power. This practice strengthens your faith and creates a sense of peace that surpasses our understanding.

Evenings provide a unique opportunity to reflect on God's faithfulness. Ending your day with declarations of gratitude reinforces a heart of thankfulness and prepares you for a restful sleep. Verses like Psalm 4:8, "I will both lie down in peace, and sleep; For You alone, O Lord, make me dwell in safety," remind you that God's protection is constant, even through the night. When you express gratitude for His guidance and provision, you close your day with a renewed sense of trust and peace.

Sarah, a young mother battling severe anxiety, shared her testimony on FaithJourney.org. Each morning, she began declaring 2 Timothy 1:7 "For God has not given us a spirit of fear, but of power and of love and of a sound mind." At first, the words felt mechanical, but as she continued to speak them daily, they began to resonate deeply. Over time, the crippling fear that had paralyzed her was replaced with a sense of calm and confidence. Sarah found herself more present with her family, excelling at work, and embracing opportunities she once avoided. Her story is a powerful reminder of how daily declarations can transform your circumstances and your heart and mind.

To build this habit effectively, consider creating a personal decree journal. In this journal, write down Scriptures that resonate with your current needs or season of life. Adapt these verses into personalized declarations. If you're seeking wisdom, Proverbs 3:5-6 is a great starting point, "Trust in the Lord with all your heart, and lean not on your own understanding; in all your ways acknowledge Him, and He shall direct your paths." Writing and speaking this verse transforms it from a written promise into a spoken declaration of faith.

Including your family in this practice can be transformative as well. Speaking blessings over your home fosters unity and creates a spiritual covering for your household. Declaring Joshua 24:15, "But as for me and my house, we will serve the Lord," reinforces a commitment to faith and establishes your home as a place of peace and protection.

Daily declarations are about more than words, it's the spiritual alignment they create. Speaking God's promises each day transforms your mindset, renews your faith, and equips you to face life's challenges with confidence. Romans 12:2 reminds us, "And do not be conformed to this world, but be transformed by the renewing of your mind, that you may prove what is that good and acceptable and perfect will of God." This renewal occurs when we consistently fill our hearts and minds with God's truth.

As you establish this routine, you will notice a shift in your life. Fear gives way to peace, doubt is replaced with faith, and opportunities seem to align with God's purpose for you. The simple yet powerful act of speaking life daily opens the door for His divine protection and blessings to flow abundantly.

Decrees for Divine Protection

The Bible is rich with promises of protection that believers can confidently declare over their lives. These Scriptures form the foundation for decrees that shield us from harm and provide peace in times of trouble. Protective decrees are never about commanding God it is the act of agreeing with His Word, speaking His promises, and activating His divine protection over our lives.

One of the most well-known passages is found in Psalm 91, often called the *Psalm of Protection*. Verse 2 says, "I will say of the Lord, 'He is my refuge and my fortress; My God, in Him I will trust." This verse sets an example of a protective decree and acknowledges God as our refuge and fortress. When you declare this truth, you remind yourself of His unshakable power and place your trust in His care.

Similarly, Isaiah 54:17 provides a powerful assurance, "No weapon formed against you shall prosper, and every tongue which rises against you in judgment You shall condemn. this is the heritage of the servants of the Lord, and their righteousness is from Me," says the Lord. When spoken aloud, this verse becomes a decree of divine security, affirming that no attack, physical, spiritual, or emotional, can succeed against those who walk in covenant with God.

Another foundational verse for protection is Proverbs 18:10: "The name of the Lord is a strong tower, the righteous run to it and are safe." Decreeing this verse is an act of faith, reminding us that God's name is a source of safety and strength. It is a declaration that we are secure within His mighty presence.

Examples of Protective Decrees in the Bible

The Bible provided many examples of individuals who experienced God's protection through spoken decrees or expressions of faith. These examples inspire us and show us how decrees can be used to activate God's promises.

1. **David's confidence in God's protection:** David often declared God's protection over his life, even in the face of overwhelming danger. In Psalm 23:4, he decrees, "Yea, though I walk through the valley of the shadow of death, I will fear no evil: for thou art with me; thy rod and thy staff they comfort me" This declaration reflects David's truth in God's guidance and presence, even in the most perilous circumstances. Speaking this verse as a decree reinforces the truth that God walks with us through every challenge, providing comfort and protection.

2. **Jehoshaphat's declarations in battle:** In 2 Chronicles 20, King Jehoshaphat faced a vast army that threatened to overwhelm Judah. In verse 12, he declared, "For we have no power giant this great multitude that is coming against us; nor do we know what to do, but our eyes are upon You." This humble declaration of reliance on God's power led to a miraculous victory. God caused confusion among the enemy forces, and Judah was delivered without needing to fight. This story teaches us the power of acknowledging our dependence on God and declaring His sovereignty over our circumstances.

3. **Jesus calming the storm:** In Mark 4:39, Jesus exemplifies the power of spoken decrees when He rebukes the wind and commands the sea, "Peace, be still!" Instantly, the storm subsided. This moment demonstrates the authority believers have through faith to speak peace and protection in tumultuous situations. While we may not calm literal storms,

we can decree peace and safety over our lives, trusting in God's power to intervene.

Practical Examples of Protective Decrees

Building protective decrees into your daily life is a proactive way to embrace God's promises. These declarations can cover various areas, from personal safety to protection for loved ones. Below are examples of decrees rooted in Scripture.

1. **Personal protection:** Psalm 91:10-11, "I decree that the Lord is my refuge and my fortress. No harm shall befall me, and no plague shall come near my dwelling, for He has given His angels charge over me to keep me in all my ways."

2. **Protection for the family:** Psalm 121:8, "I decree that my family is covered by the blood of Jesus. The Lord will preserve our going out and our coming in from this time forth and forevermore."

3. **Protection in uncertain times:** Isaiah 54:17 and Proverbs 3:6, "I decree that no weapon formed against me shall prosper. The Lord is my shield and my defender. He goes before me and makes my paths straight."

Speaking these decrees daily reinforces your trust in God's promises and creates a spiritual hedge of protection.

A powerful testimony comes from a woman named Carla, who shared her story on a Christian blog. While driving through a severe storm, she felt an overwhelming sense of fear as strong winds threatened to overturn her car. Remembering Psalm 91, she began declaring aloud, "He shall give His angels charge over you, to keep you in all your ways." Despite the dangerous experienced tornado-like winds. she credits her safe passage to God's protective hand, activated through her decree of faith.

This story illustrates how protective decrees can bring peace and deliverance in moments of fear and uncertainty. When we speak God's Word, we align ourselves with His power and invite His intervention in our lives.

As 2 Corinthians 10:4-5 states, "For the weapons of our warfare are not carnal but mightily in God for pulling down strongholds, casting down arguments and every high thing that exalts itself against the knowledge of God, bringing every thought into captivity to the obedience of Christ." Decrees are a spiritual weapon, equipping us to stand firm against fear, danger, and attack.

Decrees for Blessings and Favor

The God of the Bible is a God of abundance, overflowing with blessings and favor for His children. As believers, we are not meant to merely survive life's challenges but to thrive in the fullness of His promises. From the very beginning, God established blessings as a key part of His relationship with humanity. In Genesis 1:28, the Bible says, "Then God blessed them, and God said to them, 'Be fruitful and multiply; fill the earth and subdue it; have dominion over the fish of the sea, over the birds of the air, and over every living thing that moves on the earth," This first act of blessing shows God's heart to empower His people to flourish in every area of life.

Blessings and favor are gifts from God, freely given yet activated by faith. To walk in His favor; you must first believe that it is His desire for you. Jeremiah 29:11 assures us of God's intentions, saying, "For I know the thoughts that I think toward you, say the Lord, thoughts of peace and not of evil, to give you a future and a hope." Decrees for favor align your thoughts and words with God's plans, allowing His peace and provision to flow into your life.

Favor can be defined as God's divine influence on your behalf. It is the open doors, unexpected opportunities, and unmerited grace that distinguish God's people. As Psalm 5:12 declares, "For You, O Lord, will bless the righteous; with favor, You will surround him as with a shield." Favor surrounds you, protecting and advancing you in ways that natural effort cannot.

When you speak God's favor over your life, you are not manipulating circumstances; you are declaring His promises, trusting Him to bring them to fruition. Before starting your day, you might say: "Father, I thank You that Your favor surrounds me like a shield today. You guide my steps, and Your goodness goes before me." These words are simple but powerful, inviting God to lead and bless you in every situation.

How to Command Blessings in Daily Life

To command blessings is to intentionally speak God's promises with faith and authority. This practice is rooted in Proverbs 18:21, which says, "Death and life are in the power of the tongue, and those who love it will eat its fruit." When you choose to speak life, you align yourself with God's creative power, bringing His will into your circumstances.

Begin each day by acknowledging God's role as your provider. When you thank Him for what He has already done, you position yourself to receive even more. A simple prayer of gratitude can open the door to greater blessings. James 1:17, "Thank You, Lord, for Your faithfulness. Every good and perfect gift comes from You, and I trust You to meet all my needs."

Focus your decree over specific areas of your life. Blessings are most impactful when spoken over specific areas of your life. For example:

- **Finances:** Philippians 4:19 can be used in: "I decree that the Lord supplies all my needs according to His riches in glory by Christ Jesus."

- **Health:** Isaiah 53:5 and Psalm 103:5: "I decree that by His stripes, I am healed. The Lord restores my strength and renews my youth."

- **Family:** Joshua 24:15 and Colossians 3:15: "I decree that my household serves the Lord, and His peace reigns in our home."

Favor is God's divine advantage, enabling you to succeed beyond natural limits. By decreeing favor, you activate His supernatural influence in your life. For example:

- **In the workplace:** Psalm 90:17: "I decree that I have favor with my colleagues and superiors. The Lord blesses the work of my hands and establishes the work of my heart."

- **During difficult situations:** Isaiah 54:17: "I decree that no weapon formed against me shall prosper, and every tongue that rises against me in judgment I condemn."

- **For new opportunities:** Revelation 3:8 and Psalm 5:12: "I decree that the Lord is opening doors no man can shut, and His favor surrounds me like a shield."

To see the full impact of your decree, you must also walk in obedience to God's Word. Deuteronomy 28:1-2 says, "Now it shall come to pass, if you diligently obey the voice of the Lord your God, to observe carefully all His commandments which I command you today, that the Lord your God will set you high above all nations of the earth. And all these blessings shall come upon you and overtake you because you obey the voice of the Lord your God."

Then, every decree should end with thanksgiving. Philippians 4:6 reminds us to present our request with gratitude, saying, "Be anxious for nothing, but in everything by prayer and supplication, with thanksgiving, let your requests be made known to God." By thanking Him in advance, you demonstrate faith in His ability to fulfill His promises.

The Biblical Foundation for Blessings and Favor

1. **Blessings in the covenant with Abraham:** God's covenant with Abraham is one of the clearest examples of His desire to bless His people. In Genesis 12:2-3, God says to Abraham, "I will make you a great nation; I will bless you and make your name great, and you shall be a blessing. I will bless those who bless you, and I will curse him who curses you, and in you, all the families of the earth shall be blessed." This covenant established a pattern. God blesses His people so they can be a blessing to others. When you decree blessings, you invite God's favor into your life and position yourself to share that favor with those around you.

2. **Jesus' teaching on blessings:** In the New Testament, Jesus continues this theme, emphasizing the spiritual blessings available to those who follow Him. In Matthew 5:3-12, the Beatitudes reveal the attitudes and behaviors that lead to blessings. For example, "Blessed are the meek, for they shall

inherit the earth." Decreeing blessings in these areas invites God's kingdom into your daily life.

3. **God's favor on His chosen people:** Throughout Scripture, we see individuals marked by God's favor. From Joseph, who rose to power in Egypt despite his brothers' betrayal, to Ester, who saved her people through the king's favor, these stories demonstrate the transformative power of divine favor. When you decree favor over your life, you align yourself with this biblical precedent, inviting God to move on your behalf.

Consider the story of Sarah, a single mother who struggled to make ends meet. After learning about the power of decrees, she began speaking blessings over her finances every morning. She would declare, "The Lord is my shepherd; I shall not want. I decree financial provision and favor over my household." Within months, Sarah experienced unexpected blessings, including a job promotion and a reduction in her monthly expenses. She credits these breakthroughs to the power of God's Word spoken in faith.

When you decree blessings and favor, you invite God's provision into your life and step into your role as His co-laborer. Speak life confidently, trusting that His Word will accomplish what it set out to do as found in Isaiah 55:11. As you make decrees a daily habit, watch how God's promises transform your reality and bring you into a deeper relationship with Him.

As you embrace the transformative power of daily decrees for blessing and favor, you'll witness God's hand moving in our lives in extraordinary ways. These declarations are for personal breakthroughs and can serve as a foundation for impacting those you love and shaping the legacy you want to leave behind. Now that you've seen how decrees can unlock divine provision and supernatural favor, it's time to turn your attention outward to your family and the generations to come. In the next chapter, we will explore how to decree over your family and future, speaking God's promises into their lives and securing his guidance and protection for years ahead.

Chapter 7:

Decreeing Over Your Family

and Future

Train up a child in the way he should go, and when he is old he will not depart from it. –Proverbs 22:6

The words you speak over your family and future carry profound power. Every decree you make is a seed planted into the spiritual atmosphere, capable of shaping destinies and transforming lives. As believers, we are called to steward our own faith and the spiritual well-being of those entrusted to us. These include our spouses, children, and even future generations. This chapter will explore how to declare God's promises over your loved ones, ensuring His guidance and protection. We'll also delve into how prophetic decrees can align your path with God's divine plan, allowing you to step boldly into the future He has designed for you.

The spiritual health of your family is a reflection of the words spoken in their lives. Decreeing life, love, and unity over your household is one of the most powerful ways to cultivate a Christ-centered environment. These declarations become a shield against division and fear, replacing them with peace and purpose. In the same way, speaking God's truth over your future opens doors that no man can shut, positioning you for blessings and breakthroughs.

Whether you're seeking to restore unity in your marriage, guide your children into God's purpose, or align your life with His plan, decrees provide a spiritual roadmap. This chapter invites you to partner with God's promises, shaping your present reality and the legacy you leave behind.

Speaking Life Over Your Loved Ones

Joshua 24:15 confirms, "But as for me and my house, we will serve the Lord." Families are a reflection of God's heart. With a family, love, faith, and unity take root, providing strength in times of adversity. However, no family is immune to challenges. Whether it's marital strain, rebellious children, or conflict within the household, difficulties can overshadow God's divine plan for family life. The good news is that through prophetic decrees, we can align our words with God's promises, bringing restoration and blessing into our homes.

When you speak life over your loved ones, you're declaring God's truth into situations that seem hopeless. Your decrees are weapons of faith that can break chains of divisions that seem hopeless, heal broken relationships, and build a spiritual hedge of protection around your family. Declarations rooted in Scripture set a new spiritual tone for your household, inviting God's presence and power to intervene.

Decrees for Marriage

Marriage is the foundation of the family and a sacred covenant ordained by God. Like any relationship, it requires effort, intentionality, and divine intervention to thrive. Yet, many couples find themselves at odds due to miscommunication, external pressures, or spiritual attacks. Speaking life over your marriage can create the fortification needed to restore intimacy and love.

When you declare God's promises over your marriage, you build spiritual strength that overcomes adversity. Example:

- I decree that our marriage is rooted in God's love, unshakable and eternal. We are patient and kind to one another, building each other up in faith and love (1 Corinthians 13:4–7).

- I declare that God's wisdom guides our decisions, and His peace reigns in our relationship.

When you consistently declare these truths, you affirm the divine purpose of your marriage. Challenges lose their power to divide when your words create a spiritual bond grounded in Scripture.

A man, let's call him John, shared his testimony of a struggling marriage on a faith-based website (*Save My Marriage Testimonies*, 2013). After years of unresolved conflicts and near-divorce, he stumbled upon Proverbs 18:21, which says, "Death and life are in the power of the tongue." Convinced, John began decreeing life over his marriage each morning.

He declared, "My marriage will not end in failure. God is working to heal our hearts and restore our love." Over time, John and his wife began to notice small changes. Arguments gave way to understanding, and the couple rediscovered their shared faith. John attributes this transformation to God's power activated through consistent decrees.

Decrees for Children

Children are blessings from God, and as parents, you have the responsibility and privilege to speak words of faith, hope, and destiny over them. Even when challenges like behavioral issues, health concerns, or struggles with faith arise, you can declare God's promises for their lives.

When you decree over your children, you're protecting them spiritually and paving the way for them to walk in their divine calling. Example:

- I decree that my children are blessed and highly favored. They will walk with integrity and fulfill God's purpose for their lives.

- I declare that my children are taught by the Lord, and great shall be their peace (Isaiah 54:13).

- I decree that my children will resist temptation and grow in wisdom, stature, and favor with God and man (Luke 1:52).

These declarations establish a spiritual layer over your children, creating an environment where their faith can flourish and their identity in Christ can be strengthened.

A mother named Rachel shared her journey on a Christian blog about her son, who had turned away from the faith and become entangled in destructive behaviors (Rachel, 2024). Feeling helpless, Rachel began to declare Proverbs 22:6 daily: "Train up a child in the way he should go, and when he is old, he will not depart from it."

She prayed: "I decree that my son is a child of God, called to walk in righteousness. He will return to the Lord and fulfill his divine purpose." Months turned into years, but Rachel remained steadfast. Eventually, her son experienced a dramatic turnaround, recommitting his life to Christ. Rachel credits her unwavering faith and daily declarations for the restoration of her son's spiritual life.

Decrees for Family Unity

Family unity is a gift from God, but it often faces attacks from the enemy. Misunderstandings, grudges, and conflicts can erode relationships over time. Yet, through decrees, you can release God's healing and reconciliation into your household.

Speak unity over your family to address existing issues and prevent future discord with declarations like these:

- I decree that my family is bound together in love, walking in forgiveness and understanding (Colossians 3:13–14).

- I declare that my household serves the Lord, walking in peace and harmony (Joshua 24:15).

- I decree that no weapon formed against my family shall prosper, and every tongue that rises against us in judgment is condemned (Isaiah 54:17).

These declarations invite God's presence into your home, creating an atmosphere of peace and love. As you consistently speak life over your family, you'll notice relationships being mended and new levels of trust and affection emerging.

The Williams family faced years of division and tension, with siblings barely speaking to one another (Williams, 2024). Inspired by a sermon on prophetic decrees, the family matriarch began declaring unity over her household. She prayed: "I decree that my family is restored. We walk in love, grace, and understanding."

She also claimed Psalm 133:1, "Behold, how good and how pleasant it is for brethren to dwell together in unity." Slowly, relationships began to heal. Family members who hadn't spoken in years reconciled, and holiday gatherings became joyful occasions.

Declaring God's promises over your loved ones is a daily act of faith. Through consistent decrees, you can shape your family's spiritual atmosphere, ensuring that your household becomes a place of love, joy, and faith. Each word spoken in alignment with Scripture builds a spiritual legacy for future generations.

Shaping Your Future Through Declarations

Jeremiah 29:11 tells us, "For I know the thoughts that I think toward you, says the Lord, thoughts of peace and not of evil, to give you a future and a hope." Your future is not left to chance or dictated by circumstances. God has a specific plan for your life, filled with purpose, hope, and blessings. However, fulfilling that divine destiny often requires active participation. One of the most powerful ways to partner with God is through prophetic decrees that align your life with His Word and His will.

Prophetic declarations are more than hopeful statements. They are authoritative words that declare God's truth into your life, shaping your path and redirecting you toward His intended purpose. Through your words, you can activate God's promises, break off limitations, and propel yourself into the destiny He has prepared for you.

Every word you speak carries weight, either building up or tearing down. The Bible reminds us about it in Proverbs 18:21. When you speak life-giving words grounded in Scripture, you release God's power to work in your circumstances. For example, if you feel stuck in a season of uncertainty, you can declare the following:

- I decree that the steps of a good man are ordered by the Lord (Psalm 37:23).

- I declare that God's plans for my life are unfolding, and I walk in His divine purpose.

Such decrees are not wishful thinking; they are rooted in faith and the assurance that God's Word is true. Speaking these truths consistently begins to shift your mindset and align your reactions with God's will, opening doors to opportunities and blessings.

How Declarations Shape Your Destiny

God's promises are often activated by faith, and faith comes by hearing the Word of God as confirmed in Romans 19:17. When you declare His Word over your future, you reaffirm His promises and build your faith to believe in the impossible.

Decrees also help you overcome fear, doubt, and obstacles that try to derail your destiny. By declaring God's promises, you silence the lies of the enemy and renew your confidence in His plan. For instance, if you're unsure about your calling, you can decree the following:

- I declare that I am fearfully and wonderfully made, equipped with every spiritual gift to fulfill my purpose (Psalm 139:14).

- I decree that no weapon formed against me shall prosper, and every tongue which rises against me in judgment is condemned (Isaiah 54:17).

These declarations remind you of your identity in Christ and the victory you have through Him, enabling you to move forward with boldness and assurance.

A woman named Susan struggled to find her career path after graduating from college. She felt lost and overwhelmed, unsure of where to turn (Green, 2024). During a sermon, she heard her pastor emphasize the importance of declaring God's promises over her future. Inspired, Susan began decreeing Jeremiah 29:11 daily: "For I know that thoughts that I think toward you, says the Lord, thoughts of peace and not of evil, to give you a future and a hope."

She also declared: "I decree that God is making my path clear and leading me into a career that aligns with His purpose." Within months, doors began to open. Susan was offered a position that perfectly suited her skills and passion, a job she now sees as a direct answer to her declarations of faith.

Declaring Breakthrough During Uncertain Times

In times of uncertainty, declaring God's promises helps anchor your faith and provide clarity. Life often presents a crossroads where the path forward is unclear. Instead of succumbing to fear, prophetic decrees allow you to invite divine wisdom into your decision-making process. Example:

- If you're uncertain about a career decision, decree Psalm 23:1-3: "I declare that the Lord is my Shepherd; I shall not want. He leads me beside the still waters and restores my soul." This declaration invites God's peaceful guidance, reminding you that He will direct your steps.

- When faced with a significant life decision, decree Psalm 37:23: "The steps of a good man are ordered by the Lord, and He delights in his way." This affirms your trust in God's ability to lead you according to His perfect will.

By speaking these declarations, you shift your focus from uncertainty to God's sovereignty, allowing Him to lead you into His best for your life.

Overcoming Limiting Beliefs With Declarations

Sometimes, the greatest obstacles to your destiny are the lies you've believed about yourself. Prophetic declarations combat these lies by affirming our indemnity in Christ and the truth of God's Word. Example:

- If you struggle with feelings of inadequacy, decree Psalm 139:14: "I am fearfully and wonderfully made; marvelous are Your works, and that my soul knows very well."

- When doubt clouds your ability to fulfill God's calling, decree Philippians 4:13: "I can do all things through Christ who strengthens me."

These declarations renew your mind, helping you break free from self-doubt and walk confidently into the destiny God has designed for you.

Declaring Breakthrough in Challenging Times

Life's challenges often seem like insurmountable mountains, but God has equipped you with His Word to declare victory over every situation. Prophetic decrees are a way to claim the breakthrough you need, whether in relationships, finances, or personal growth. Example:

- If you're facing financial struggles, decree Philippians 3:19: "The Lord shall supply all my need according to His riches in glory by Christ Jesus." This declaration reinforces your faith in God's provision.

- When dealing with relationship challenges, decree Romans 8:28: "I declare that God is working all things together for my good because I love Him and am called according to His purpose."

These declarations release God's power to bring transformation and restoration to the most difficult areas of your life.

Take the story of Joseph from the bible as an example of how declaring God's promises can shape a destiny. Joseph faced betrayal, slavery, and imprisonment, yet he held on to the dream God had given him. His unwavering faith and declarations of God's favor carried him through every trial. Eventually, Joseph was elevated to a position of influence in Egypt, fulfilling God's plan for his life (Genesis 37:50).

In modern times, consider the testimony of a man named Daniel, who struggled with unemployment. Daniel began declaring Psalm 37:25: "I have been young, and now am old, yet I have to see the righteous forsaken, nor his descendants begging bread." Within weeks, he received a job offer that met his financial needs and aligned with his skills and passion. Daniel's prophetic declarations reminded him of God's faithfulness and kept his faith strong in challenging times.

Speaking Into the Future

Prophetic decrees can address present needs and shape the future. When you declare God's promises over your life, you set the foundation for what's to come.

- For a future filled with purpose, decree Jeremiah 29:11: "I declare that God's plans for me are good, to give me a future and a hope."

- For boldness and confidence in your calling, decree 2 Timothy 1:7: "I declare that God has not given me a spirit of fear, but of power, love, and a sound mind."

These declarations create a positive and faith-filled trajectory, guiding you toward the destiny God has ordained for you.

Align With God's Timing and Will

Timing is crucial in fulfilling God's plan for us. Prophetic declarations align your life with His timing and will, helping you avoid unnecessary delays caused by doubt or disobedience. Decree Isaiah 40:31 that reminds you to trust in His perfect plan:

- I declare that I will wait on the Lord and renew my strength. I will mount up with wings like eagles, run and not be weary, walk and not faint."

Declarations help you walk confidently in the assurance that His timing is always right, even when the journey requires patience and perseverance.

As you continue to embrace the power of prophetic decrees, you are shaping your personal destiny and that of your family. Best of all, you are positioning yourself to impact the world around you. The words you speak have the capacity to ripple beyond your immediate sphere, touching lives and transforming communities. Just as God calls individuals to steward their personal lives, He also calls believers to unite their voices in faith, declaring His will over cities, nations, and the world.

In the next chapter, we will explore the dynamic potential of corporate decrees, when believers come together with one heart and one voice to proclaim God's truth. We'll uncover how a united declaration can bring about community transformation, break spiritual strongholds, and invite divine intervention on a larger scale. Let us step into this greater calling and discover how your voice, joined with others, can usher in God's kingdom on earth.

Chapter 8:

Corporate Decrees and

Community Transformation

Again I say to you that if two of you agree on earth concerning anything that they ask, it will be done for them by My Father in heaven. –Matthew 18:19

There is an extraordinary power in unity. When believers come together to decree God's truth, the effects can be extraordinary. Jesus promised that where two or more gather in His name and agree in prayer, Heaven will listen and respond. Corporate decrees harness this principle, combining the faith and voices of many to release God's will onto communities, nations, and the world.

This chapter invites you to explore the transformative potential of united declarations. Corporate decrees allow the body of Christ to rise with one voice, breaking spiritual strongholds, releasing healing, and calling down revival. These declarations are acts of faith that echo

Heaven's intentions, shaking the spiritual atmosphere and paving the way for lasting change.

The Power of United Decrees

The power of united decrees lies in the agreement and faith of God's people coming together as one. When believers align their hearts and voices in unity, they tap into the promise of divine intervention. The Bible repeatedly demonstrates the power of collective prayer and proclamation, showing us that when we unite in purpose and faith, spiritual strongholds can be broken, communities can be healed, and nations can experience revival.

One of the most striking examples of the power of united decrees can be found in the story of Jehoshaphat in 2 Chronicles 20:15. Faced with a vast army threatening Judah, King Jehoshaphat called the nation together to seek God. As the people prayed and declared their dependence on the Lord, the Spirit of God spoke through Jahaziel, saying, "Do not be afraid nor dismayed because of this great multitude, for the battle, is not yours, but God's"

In response, the people praised God with a loud voice, and their unified worship became a powerful declaration of faith. The result? God set ambushes against their enemies, and Judah emerged victorious without lifting a sword. This account shows that when God's people unite in faith and proclamation, Heaven moves on their behalf.

Another example is found in the early church. In Acts 4:23-31, after Peter and John were released from prison, the believers gathered to pray together. They declared God's sovereignty and asked for boldness to continue preaching the gospel. Their united prayers and declarations shook the place where they were gathered, and they were all filled with the Holy Spirit. This united decree empowered the early church to move forward with boldness and effectiveness, spreading the gospel despite intense opposition.

A modern-day example of the power of united decrees comes from the city of Manchester, Kentucky. In the early 2000s, the community was plagued by poverty, drug addiction, and crime. Local churches came together for a united prayer movement known as "The Manchester Awakening" (Lawrence, 2024). Believers from across denominations began to decree God's promises over their city, declaring Isaiah 61:1–3 "The Spirit of the Lord God is upon Me because the Lord has anointed Me to preach good tidings to the poor; He has sent Me to heal the brokenhearted, to proclaim liberty to the captives..."

The results were nothing short of miraculous. Drug dealers were arrested, addiction rates plummeted, and the community experienced a spiritual and social revival. The story was even documented in the film *Appalachian Dawn*, illustrating how united decrees and prayer can transform an entire city.

United decrees are powerful because they align with God's design for the church as a body. Ephesians 4:16 describes how the church functions as one unit: "...from whom the whole body, joined and knit together by what every joint supplies, according to the effective working by which every part does its share, causes growth of the body for the edifying of itself in love." When believers unite in faith and purpose, their declarations amplify, carrying greater spiritual weight.

These decrees also draw upon the promise of Matthew 18:19: "Again I say to you that if two of you agree on earth concerning anything that they ask, it will be done for them by My Father in heaven." Agreement magnifies faith and creates an atmosphere where God's power can manifest more tangibly.

The Impact of Corporate Declarations in a Church or Community Setting

Corporate declarations in a church or community setting have a profound and transformative impact. When believers come together to proclaim God's promises and align their voices with His Word, the spiritual atmosphere shifts. These united declarations create a ripple effect, influencing individual lives and the entire community. From creating unity within the church to breaking spiritual strongholds in a region, corporate declarations wield a power that reflects the heart of God's Kingdom.

The Bible consistently highlights the power of communal prayer and declarations. In 2 Chronicles 7:14, God gives a powerful promise: "If My people who are called by My name will humble themselves, and pray and seek My face, and turn from their wicked ways, then I will hear from heaven, and will forgive their sin and heal their land."

This verse emphasizes that the collective actions and declarations of God's people can lead to national healing and restoration. It's not the isolated prayers of one person but the unified cries of a community that moves Heaven to respond.

Another striking example is the story of Jonah and the city of Nineveh (Jonah 3:5–10). When Jonah declared God's warning of impending judgment, the entire city, from the king to the common people, responded with fasting, prayer, and declarations of repentance. Their unified response caused God to relent in bringing disaster upon them.

This account demonstrates the incredible potential of corporate repentance and declarations to change the fate of the community.

The Power of Agreement

In Redding, California, Bethel Church has become known for its focus on declarations and community transformation. The church often engages in corporate declarations for healing and revival, aligning its faith with God's promises. In one documented instance, the church united in prayer and declaration over a young girl named Olive who had tragically passed away.

Although the outcome was not what they had hoped for, the global unity in prayer and declaration brought people together in faith and hope, creating a renewed passion for God's power of love (*Bethel Church | On Earth as It Is in Heaven*, 2019). This example shows that even when the desired result isn't immediately visible, corporate declarations strengthen faith and build a community that believes in God's ability to intervene.

Breaking Strongholds in a Community

Corporate declarations are especially effective in breaking spiritual strongholds over a region. For example, in 1995, pastors and leaders in Cali, Colombia, organized a citywide prayer gathering to confront the pervasive influence of drug cartels (*1995 Cali, Colombia Revival*, 2021). They declared God's justice, peace, and righteousness over their city, citing Scriptures such as Psalm 33:12: "Blessed is the nation whose God is the Lord, the people He has chosen as His own inheritance."

The results were astonishing. Within months, crime rates dropped, drug cartels were dismantled, and the city experienced a spiritual revival. This event, often referred to as the "Cali Revival," shows us how corporate declarations can bring tangible change to a community.

Unity and Vision in the Church

In a church setting, corporate declarations unite the congregation under a shared vision and purpose. When a church declares God's promises together, it fosters a sense of unity and shared faith. This unity is vital for the church to function as the body of Christ (1 Corinthians 12:12-27).

Corporate declarations also help the church align with God's mission. For example, a church declaring Isaiah 61:1–3 can focus on bringing hope to the brokenhearted, freedom to the captives, and comfort to those who mourn. These declarations inspire the congregation and set the spiritual direction for the church's ministries.

Examples of Corporate Decrees

Corporate decrees serve as spiritual acts of unity, aligning a group of believers with Heaven's agenda. These decrees carry immense power because they amplify faith through collective agreement. As Jesus said in Matthew 18:19, if two agree on earth our Father in heaven will hear and answer our prayer.

When believers unite in declarations, their voices resonate with the authority of Heaven, causing spiritual shifts that bring tangible results. This section explores how corporate declarations can ignite revival, heal communities, and transform nations, offering biblical and real-life examples to inspire and guide.

Declarations for Revival

Revival is often born from hunger for God and nurtured by collective faith. When a group of believers comes together to declare God's promises, they create an atmosphere ripe for His Spirit to move. Revival begins in the heart but becomes contagious when proclaimed over a region.

The revival led by Johah in Nineveh offers a profound biblical example. Despite being a reluctant prophet, Johah delivered a message of repentance, and the people of Nineveh responded with fasting and declarations of faith.

In Jonah 3:10, it is written, "Then God saw their works, that they turned from their evil way; and God relented from the disaster that He had said He would bring upon them, and He did not do it." This demonstrates how a united response, accompanied by declarations of repentance and faith, can lead to divine intervention and revival.

One of the most remarkable modern-day examples is the Azusa Street Revival of 1906. What began as a small prayer meeting in Los Angeles grew into a global movement of revival and renewal (*The Azusa Street Revival*, n.d.). The leaders and participants often declared Acts 2:17: "And it shall come to pass in the last days, says God, that I will pour out of My Spirit on all flesh; your sons and your daughters shall prophesy, your young men shall see visions, your old men shall dream dreams."

These declarations set the tone for a movement that changed the spiritual landscape of the 20th century, bringing countless people to Christ.

In the 21st century, gatherings like The Send, which unite believers to pray and declare over their cities, have sparked similar movements.

Participants declare verses like Isaiah 6:8: "Also I heard the voice of the Lord, saying: 'Whom shall I send, and who will go for Us?" Then I said, 'Here am I! Send me.'"

Practical Application

To declare revival in your community, consider these steps:

1. **Unite with others:** Gather a group of believers to pray and proclaim God's promises for revival.

2. **Use Scripture:** Base your declarations on verses such as Hosea 6:2: "After two days He will revive us; on the third day He will raise us up, that we may live in His sight."

3. **Declare boldly:** Speak with confidence, proclaiming, "Our city will experience a move of God like never before!"

When you align your heart and voice with Heaven, you can create the spiritual conditions for revival to take root in our community.

Declarations for Community Healing

Communities often bear the scars of division, poverty, and violence, but united declarations can usher in God's healing power. Speaking life and restoration over neighborhoods creates an environment where change becomes possible.

Jeremiah's prayer for the welfare of Babylon offers a timeless principle. Jeremiah 29:7 confirms, "And seek the peace of the city when I have caused you to be carried away captive, and pray to the Lord for it; for in its peace you will have peace."

This command was given to exiled Israelites, reminding them that their prayers and proclamations could bless even a foreign land.

Another powerful example is found in Nehemiah, who prayed and declared over Jerusalem's broken walls. Nehemiah 4:20 highlights his faith: "Wherever you hear the sound of the trumpet, rally to us there, our God will fight for us." Through unity and bold declarations, the walls were rebuilt, and the community was restored.

In 2018, following devastating wildfires in California, churches in affected areas united to proclaim God's restoration, (Smith, 2018). Using Scriptures like Isaiah 61:3, "To console those who mourn in Zion, to give them beauty for ashes, the oil of joy for mourning, the garment of praise for the spirit of heaviness," they declared God's promise of rebuilding and hope.

Over time, their declarations bore fruit as neighborhoods began to heal, families were restored, and new opportunities emerged.

Practical Application

To declare community healing, follow these steps:

1. **Identify key issues:** Pinpoint areas where healing is needed, such as poverty, crime, or division.

2. **Gather in unity:** Bring together believers to pray and declare over the community.

3. **Proclaim specific declarations:** Examples:

   a. We declare that peace will reign in our streets!

   b. We proclaim restoration over broken families and relationships.

Through faith-filled proclamations, you can sow seeds of hope and transformation in your community.

Declarations for National Transformation

The impact of corporate decrees extends beyond local communities to entire nations. When believers unite to declare God's purpose over their land, they invite His righteousness and justice to prevail.

The story of Esther demonstrates how united action and decrees can save a nation. Esther 4:16 records her bold words: "Go, gather all the Jews who are present in Shushan, and fast for me; neither eat nor drink for three days, night or day. My maids and I will fast likewise. And so I will go to the king, which is against the law; and if I perish, I perish!"

Through her leadership and the united prayers and declarations of her people, the Jewish nation was saved from destruction. Another example is found in 2 Chronicles 7:14: "If My people who are called by My name will humble themselves, and pray and seek My face, and turn from their wicked ways, then I will hear from heaven, and will forgive their sin and heal their land."

This verse remains a foundational promise for those who seek national revival and transformation.

Practical Application

To declare transformation over your nation, do the following:

1. **Pray for leaders:** Use Scriptures like 1 Timothy 2:1–2: "Therefore I exhort first of all that supplications, prayers,

intercessions, and giving of thanks be made for all men, for kings and all who are in authority."

2. **Declare righteousness:** Proclaim verses like Psalm 33:12: "Blessed is the nation whose God is the Lord, the people He has chosen as His own inheritance."

3. **Unite across denominations:** Encourage churches to come together, setting aside differences to declare God's purposes over the land.

Through corporate decrees, believers can see God's power released in extraordinary ways. From local revivals to national transformations, the unity of faith-filled declarations has the potential to shape history and bring Heaven to earth.

The power of corporate decrees is undeniable, transforming both individuals and entire communities and nations. When believers come together in unity, their collective voice becomes a force that can change spiritual atmospheres and bring Heaven's will into earthly realities. These declarations for revival, healing, and transformation demonstrate the authority we have as the Body of Christ to speak life, restoration, and hope into every corner of our world.

However, as we step boldly into the practice of decreeing, we often encounter resistance. Opposition arises, whether in the form of internal doubts, external challenges, or spiritual warfare. In the next chapter, we will learn to stand firm, speak God's truth with authority, and witness His victory in the face of adversity.

Chapter 9:

Overcoming Opposition

With Decrees

No weapon formed against you shall prosper, and every tongue which rises against you in judgment you shall condemn. This is the heritage of the servants of the Lord, and their righteousness is from Me, says the Lord. —Isaiah 54:17

Opposition is inevitable when you walk in faith and declare God's promises over your life, family, and community. The enemy seeks to undermine your confidence, sow seeds of doubt, and disrupt the plans God has for you. But you are not without weapons in this spiritual battle. Decrees rooted in Scripture become a powerful tool, allowing you to claim victory even amidst fierce resistance.

In this chapter, we discover the role of prophetic declarations in spiritual warfare. You'll discover how to use decrees to dismantle spiritual attacks, break through barriers, and stand firm in the face of adversity. When you are facing personal trials or larger spiritual battles, you can protect yourself and learn how to release words of power that align with God's promises. You will learn how to strengthen your declarations for every challenge. The same authority that silenced storms, healed the sick, and brought deliverance in biblical times is available to you today. Let's explore how to wield it boldly and effectively.

Decrees in Spiritual Warfare

Spiritual warfare is an undeniable reality of the believer's life. The Bible teaches us that our struggle is not against flesh and blood but against spiritual forces of darkness (Ephesians 6:12). In these battles, decrees are a weapon of authority given by God to counteract the enemy's plans. When we declare God's Word, we are not merely speaking into the air; we are releasing divine truths that dismantle lies, destroy strongholds, and establish God's will.

The example of Jesus in the wilderness confirms the power of spoken decrees in spiritual warfare. When Satan tempted Him, Jesus did not engage in debate or argument. Instead, as found in Matthew 4:4-10, He countered each temptation by declaring, "It is written," followed by Scripture. Each decree silenced the enemy and affirmed God's truth.

Similarly, David faced spiritual and physical opposition when confronting Goliath. Before the battle even began, David made a bold decree (Samuel 17:46): "This day the Lord will deliver you into my hand." His words were not based on his strength but on God's power and promise. David's decree changed the spiritual atmosphere, leading to victory.

In our lives, spiritual warfare may manifest as persistent fear, confusion, or discouragement. These attacks can leave us feeling powerless, but decrees remind us of the authority we have in Christ. Declaring verses such as 2 Corinthians 19:4–5, "For the weapons of our warfare are not carnal but mighty in God for pulling down strongholds," enables us to refocus on God's power to overcome.

A woman named Sarah shared her testimony on a Christian blog about battling anxiety (Brown, 2017). She felt consumed by fear, unable to sleep or function normally. Inspired by her pastor's sermon on spiritual warfare, she began declaring Philippians 4:7: "The peace of God, which surpasses all understanding, will guard your hearts and minds through Christ Jesus."

Daily, she spoke this truth over herself: "I decree that God's peace guards my heart and mind. Anxiety has no place in my life. My mind is sound, and my spirit is calm." Over time, she noticed a shift. The panic attacks ceased, and she experienced God's peace in tangible ways. Her testimony is a powerful reminder that decrees are effective weapons in spiritual warfare.

Using Declarations to Overcome Spiritual Attacks

Spiritual attacks are often subtle, aiming to weaken our faith and disconnect us from God. You might be facing an attack on your health, finances, relationships, or mind, declarations provide a way to fight back. When you align your words with God's promises, you reclaim the territory that your enemy seeks to steal.

The Apostle Paul's exhortation in Ephesians 6:17 provides the "sword of the Spirit, which is the Word of God," as part of the believer's armor. This sword becomes active when spoken. Declarations cut through lies, bringing clarity and victory. For instance, when fear threatens to overwhelm, declaring Psalm 27:1, "The Lord is my light and my salvation; whom shall I fear?" reaffirms God's protection and power.

Paul and Silas experienced a spiritual attack when they were beaten and imprisoned unjustly. Instead of succumbing to despair, they responded by praying and singing hymns to God, a form of declaration in Acts 16:25. Their words shifted the atmosphere, leading to a miraculous earthquake that opened the prison doors and loosened their chains. This example teaches us that declarations are defensive and also offensive. They invite God's intervention, creating opportunities for His power to manifest.

A man named Robert shared his testimony about facing financial difficulties after losing his job (GodUpdates, 2024). Bills piled up, and he felt defeated. But instead of giving in to despair, Robert began declaring God's provision. Using Deuteronomy 28:12, "The Lord will open to you His good treasure, the heavens, to give the rain to you land in its season," he declared, "I declare that God is my provider. He opens the heavens to bless me with abundance."

Within weeks, Robert experienced unexpected breakthroughs: a job offer with better pay and financial help from an old friend. His testimony underscores the transformative power of declarations during spiritual attacks.

Practical Steps for Using Declarations

When you use declarations in spiritual warfare, you align yourself with the truth of God's Word, dismantle the enemy's strategies, and invite

God's power to operate in your life. These spoken truths are a lifeline, pulling you out of darkness and into the light of His victory.

1. **Identify the attack:** Recognize the area where the enemy is working. Is it fear, scarcity, or relationship strife?

2. **Find relevant scriptures:** Search for verses that address the specific issue. For example, declare Isaiah 41:10 for fear: "Fear not, for I am with you; be not dismayed, for I am your God."

3. **Speak with authority:** Declarations carry the authority of God's Word. Speak them boldly, believing they will accomplish what they say. Isaiah 55:11: "So shall My words be that goes forth from My mouth; it shall not return to Me void, but it shall accomplish what I please, and it shall prosper in the thing for which I sent it."

4. **Persist in faith:** The enemy may not retreat immediately. Continue declaring God's promises until you see the breakthrough.

Standing Firm in the Face of Adversity

Adversity is a certainty in life, but how we respond to it determines whether we emerge strengthened or defeated. The Bible repeatedly encourages believers to stand firm in faith, regardless of trials. Decrees are a powerful way to ground yourself in God's promises, enabling you to face challenges with resilience and courage.

Adversity often tests our trust in God. When the Israelites stood before the Red Sea with Pharaoh's army closing in behind them, fear and doubt surged. But Moses declared in Exodus 14:13, "Do not be afraid. Stand still, and see the salvation of the Lord, which He will accomplish for you today." His decree set the stage for God's miraculous intervention—parting the sea and delivering the Israelites from harm.

In our own lives, standing firm in adversity requires an unshakable confidence in God's faithfulness. This confidence grows as we speak His Word over our circumstances. Declarations like Isaiah 41:10, "Fear not, for I am with you; be not dismayed, for I am your God," remind us that we are never alone, even in our darkest moments.

Decrees That Strengthen and Empower

Decrees are a way to reinforce our spiritual armor. They secure our faith, anchor our hope, and provide a lens through which we view adversity. Consider the Apostle Paul's words in 2 Corinthians 4:8–9, "We are hard-pressed on every side, yet not crushed; we are perplexed, but not in despair; persecuted, but not forsaken; struck down, but not destroyed." Decrees based on this passage might include the following:

- I declare that though I face pressure, I will not be crushed. God's strength sustains me.

- I decree that despair has no hold on me; God's hope fills my heart.

- I proclaim that I am never forsaken; the Lord is with me in every trial.

These declarations encourage and empower you. They remind you of your position in Christ and the limitless resources available to you through His Spirit.

Job's story is one of profound suffering. Stripped of his wealth, health, and family, he had every reason to despair. Yet, amidst his anguish, he declared in Job 13:15, "Though He slay me, yet will I trust Him." This decree reflected Job's unwavering faith, even when he didn't understand God's plan. His declaration became a source of strength, enabling him to endure and eventually witness restoration.

A woman named Grace shared her story in an online testimony (Marshall, 2018). After losing her home in a fire, she felt devastated. Everything she worked for was gone in an instant. Instead of succumbing to despair, Grace began declaring Psalm 46:1: "God is our refuge and strength, a very present help in trouble."

Her declaration was simple: "I decree that God is my refuge. I am not abandoned; He is with me and will restore what was lost." Within months, Grace experienced unexpected blessings, including a new home provided by her church community. Her story illustrates how decrees can strengthen and empower us during trials.

Practical Steps for Standing Firm With Decrees

1. **Acknowledge the challenge:** Denial doesn't lead to victory. Face adversity with honesty and bring it before God.

2. **Choose relevant scriptures:** Select verses that speak to your situation. For financial struggles, Philippians 4:19, "My God shall supply all your need," is a powerful foundation.

3. **Declare daily:** Make decrees part of your daily routine. Speak them aloud, believing they carry divine authority.

4. **Invite community support:** Share your decrees with trusted friends or family who can stand in agreement with you.

Standing firm in adversity is not about relying on your own strength. It's about tapping into God's limitless power. Decrees remind us that trials are temporary but God's promises are eternal. As you declare His Word over your life, you'll find yourself empowered to endure and overcome, no matter what challenges come your way.

This ability to stand firm strengthens your faith and serves as a testimony to others. When they see your resilience and trust in God, it inspires them to seek Him in their own struggles. Standing firm is not just about surviving; it's about thriving in the assurance that God is with you, for you, and working all things together for your good as promised in Romans 8:28.

As we've discovered, decrees are powerful tools for overcoming opposition and standing firm in the face of trials. They align our hearts with God's truth, infuse us with courage, and empower us to face challenges with unwavering faith. Whether combating spiritual attacks or enduring life's adversities, declarations remind us of who we are in Christ and the victory we have through Him.

While life with God is about enduring, it's also about growing, advancing, and stepping boldly into His plan for us. As we transition to the next chapter, we'll focus on moving forward with confidence. We'll discover how to walk in the assurance of God's promises, using decrees to chart a path of purpose and peace for the days ahead. This is your moment to rise, trust, and embrace the abundant life He has prepared for you.

Chapter 10:

Moving Forward With Confidence

For I know the thoughts that I think toward you, says the Lord, thoughts of peace and not of evil, to give you a future and a hope. —Jeremiah 29:11

You've come a long way in understanding the power of decrees. Each chapter has been a step toward equipping you to stand firm in faith, speak God's Word boldly, and see transformation in every area of your life. But the journey doesn't end here. Moving forward means creating a lifestyle where prophetic declarations are a natural part of your daily rhythm.

This chapter will guide you on how to include decrees into your everyday life. You'll hear inspiring testimonies of those who have experienced remarkable breakthroughs by faithfully speaking God's

Word. As we draw this journey to a close, you'll receive words of encouragement to carry you into the future with confidence.

God's plans for you are good. His promises are unshakable. Together, let's step into this next phase fully equipped to speak life, declare His truth, and walk boldly into all He has for you. The best is yet to come.

Living a Lifestyle of Prophetic Decrees

Living a lifestyle of prophetic decrees is never about an occasional spiritual exercise. It is about weaving God's Word into the fabric of your everyday life. It's a mindset, a discipline, and a declaration of faith that shapes how you interact with the world around you. When you speak God's promises consistently, you align your heart, thoughts, and actions with His will. This practice transforms your circumstances and strengthens your relationship with Him.

To continue using decrees effectively, start by setting aside time each day to focus on speaking God's Word. Just as you might have a morning routine for your physical body, such as brushing your teeth or exercising, a spiritual routine strengthens your inner self. Begin your day by declaring truths over your life, your family, and your future.

For example, upon waking, you might say, "This is the day the Lord has made; I will rejoice and be glad in it (Psalm 118:24). I am the head and not the tail, I am above only and not beneath. The Lord is my shepherd; I lack nothing, His goodness and mercy follow me today and all the days of my life.

This simple practice sets the tone for your day. It fills your heart with faith and expectation, no matter what lies ahead.

Anchor Your Decree in Scripture

Consistency is vital but so is grounding your decrees in God's Word. Prophetic declarations are powerful because they are rooted in the unchanging truth of the Bible. They are powerful affirmations backed with divine truths in God's authority. Example:

- If you're seeking peace, declare Isaiah 26:3: "You will keep him in perfect peace, whose mind is stayed on You because he trusts in You.*"*

- If you need provision, proclaim Philippians 4:19: "And my God shall supply all your needs according to His riches in glory by Christ Jesus."

As you speak these promises, visualize them taking root in your life. See God's Word bringing peace to your mind, opening doors of opportunity, and providing for your needs.

Include Decrees in Daily Life

Prophetic decrees aren't limited to prayer time. Include them in everyday moments. Speak over your work, your relationships, and even mundane tasks.

- If you're driving to work, declare safety and divine favor (Psalm 121:8): "The Lord will preserve my going out and my coming in from this time forth, and even forevermore."

- If you're making a decision, decree wisdom (James 1:5): "If any of you lacks wisdom, let him ask of God, who gives to all liberally and without reproach, and it will be given to him."

This ongoing practice keeps your focus on God and creates an atmosphere of faith wherever you go.

A woman named Lisa, whose testimony was shared on FaithGateway.com, faced overwhelming financial struggles (*Lisa Whittle*, 2024). She felt paralyzed by fear and uncertainty. One day, she decided to begin speaking about her situation. Daily, she declared Scriptures like Psalm 34:10: "But those who seek the Lord shall not lack any good thing."

Over time, her mindset began to shift. She found unexpected opportunities for income and started to see God's provision in ways she hadn't anticipated. Her financial situation improved, but more importantly, her faith grew stronger. Lisa's story reminds us that daily decrees are not about quick fixes at all but about cultivating trust in God's faithfulness.

The Power of Consistency

Consistency is where the transformation happens. Like planting seeds, decrees require time and patience to bear fruit. Even when you don't see immediate results, keep speaking. Trust that God is working behind the scenes.

Consider the story of Joshua at Jericho. God instructed him and the Israelites to march around the city for seven days. They declared victory through their obedience, even before the walls fell. Their perseverance led to the miraculous collapse of Jericho's walls as found in Joshua 6.

In the same way, your consistent declarations, rooted in faith, will bring breakthroughs in God's timing. Each time you declare God's Word, do it with expectation. Picture the promises of God unfolding in our lives. Speak with confidence, knowing that His Word does not return void, as confirmed by Isaiah 55:11.

For example, when you declare healing, envision yourself as healthy and strong. When you speak peace over your family, imagine harmony and unity in your home. This faith-filled expectation aligns your spirit with God's promises.

As you commit to this lifestyle, remember that prophetic decrees speak of a relationship with God, not rituals. They draw you closer to God, helping you to trust Him more deeply. Let them become as natural as breathing. Speak His Word over your life and watch as His plans unfold.

Testimonies of Breakthroughs

Prophetic declarations are powerful tools that can transform lives when rooted in faith and God's Word. Many have experienced miraculous breakthroughs by speaking God's promises into their circumstances. These testimonies inspire and remind us that God's Word is alive, active, and able to bring change to even the most challenging situations.

Overcoming Chronic Illness

One remarkable story is that of Pastor Dodie Osteen, who was diagnosed with terminal liver cancer in the early 1980s (Osteen, 2019). Given only weeks to live, she turned to the power of God's Word. Dodie began declaring healing Scriptures over herself daily, including the following:

- Isaiah 53:5: "By His stripes, we are healed."

- Psalm 103:2–3: "Bless the Lord, O my soul, and forget not all His benefits, who forgives all your iniquities, who heals all your diseases."

Despite her grim prognosis, she refused to let her faith waver. Day by day, she continued to decree God's promises, trusting Him for her healing. Today, decades later, Dodie is still alive and cancer-free. Her story is a powerful example of how prophetic declarations, rooted in unwavering faith, can lead to miraculous breakthroughs.

Financial Breakthrough

Another inspiring testimony comes from a couple, John and Sarah, who were drowning in debt and struggling to make ends meet (*From Rags to Riches*, n.d.). They decided to take a different approach to their financial challenges by declaring Scripture about provision and abundance. They spoke verses like the following:

- Philippians 4:19: And my God shall supply all your needs according to His riches in glory by Christ Jesus.

- Deuteronomy 28:12: The Lord will open to you His good treasure, the heavens, to give the rain to your land in its season and to bless all the work of your hand.

Over time, they began to notice unexpected blessings. A promotion at work, opportunities for additional income, and unexpected financial gifts from friends and family all contributed to their financial recovery. Within two years, they were completely debt-free.

Their testimony shows us that prophetic declarations, combined with patience and faith, can soften hearts and restore what was once lost.

Restoration of Relationships

Prophetic declarations can also bring healing to broken relationships. Consider the story of a mother whose relationship with her estranged daughter had been fractured for years. Joseph Prince's website tells of the restored relationship after a period of estrangement (Prince, 2024).

143

Maria began praying and decreed reconciliation, speaking promises like the following:

- Malachi 4:6: He will turn the hearts of the parents to their children, and the hearts of the children to their parents.

- Colossians 3:13: Bear with each other and forgive one another if any of you has a grievance against someone. Forgive as the Lord forgave you.

Though there was no immediate change, Maria remained faithful in her declarations. Months later, her daughter unexpectedly reached out, seeking forgiveness and a fresh start. Their relationship was restored, and they now share a bond stronger than ever.

This testimony illustrates that prophetic declarations, combined with patience and faith, can soften hearts and restore what was once lost.

Revival in a Community Through Declarations

In 1906, during the Azusa Street Revival in Los Angeles, believers gathered to pray and decree God's promises over their city (*Azusa Street Mission*, 2024). Led by William Seymour, they declared Scriptures like the following:

- 2 Chronicles 7:14: "If My people who are called by My name will humble themselves, and pray and seek My face, and turn from their wicked ways, then I will hear from heaven, and will forgive their sin and heal their land."

- Isaiah 61: 4: "And they shall rebuild the old ruins, they shall raise up the former desolations, and they shall repair the ruined cities, the desolation of many generations."

Their faith-filled declarations sparked a spiritual awakening that spread far beyond their community. People traveled from around the world to experience the revival, which brought thousands to Christ and led to physical healings, deliverances, and the breaking of racial barriers.

This example reminds us that prophetic decrees are not limited to individual lives. They have the power to transform entire communities when believers unite in faith.

Overcoming Fear and Anxiety

Another testimony comes from a man named James who battled severe anxiety and fear (Share, 2009). After hearing a sermon on the power of declarations, he began declaring Scripture over himself daily:

- Timothy 1:7: "For God has not given us a spirit of fear, but of power and of love and of a sound mind."

- Psalm 27:1: "The Lord is my light and my salvation, whom shall I fear? The Lord is the stronghold of my life, of whom shall I be afraid?"

As James faithfully declared these promises, he noticed a gradual change. His anxiety began to lift, and he gained the courage to face situations that once paralyzed him. Today, he lives free from fear, crediting his transformation to God's Word and the practice of prophetic decrees.

These testimonies reveal the transformative power of declaring God's Word. Whether you are seeking healing, financial provision, restoration, or deliverance, God's promises are available to you. Remember that these declarations are expressions of faith that align your heart with His will.

Take inspiration from these stories and begin speaking life into your own circumstances. Trust in the God who is able to do exceedingly, abundantly above all you can ask or think (Ephesians 3:20). Keep declaring His promises and watch how He moves in your life.

Encouragement for the Journey Ahead

As we close this transformative journey through the power of prophetic decrees, let's first read Philippians 1:6: "Being confident of this very thing, that He who has begun a good work in you will complete it until the day of Jesus Christ." Let this truth anchor your heart: God is faithful to complete the work He has started in you. The declarations you have spoken are seeds of faith planted in the fertile soil of God's promises. They will bear fruit in due time, even when the path seems uncertain.

The road ahead will have its share of challenges, but you are now equipped with a powerful spiritual weapon. Your voice aligned with God's Word. Speaking life, truth, and faith over your circumstances has opened a door to divine breakthroughs. Remember, God's Word never returns void (Isaiah 55:11). Every decree spoken in faith carries heaven's authority to bring change.

Take heart, for the journey with God is one of continual growth and empowerment. As you walk forward, each declaration builds spiritual momentum. Like David facing Goliath, your decrees enable you to meet every challenge with courage, knowing that the victory belongs to the Lord (1 Samuel 17:45–47).

Your journey isn't just for you. As God transforms your life through prophetic declarations, your testimony will inspire others. When you share stories of how speaking God's Word shaped your life, you encourage others to step into the same boldness. Revelation 12:11 reminds us that "they overcame him by the blood of the Lamb and by the word of their testimony." Your experience can light the path of others to walk in freedom and blessing.

It's essential to stay the course, even when results aren't immediate. Some breakthroughs take time, but persistence is key. Galatians 6:9 urges, "And let us not grow weary while doing good, for in due season we shall reap if we do not lose heart." Keep decreeing God's promises with unwavering faith, trusting that He is working behind the scenes to fulfill them.

Let every step forward be marked by the confidence that God is with you, guiding your declarations and shaping your future. Psalm 37:23–24 assures us, "The steps of a good man are ordered by the Lord, and He delights in his way. Though he falls, he shall not be utterly cast down; for the Lord upholds him with His hand."

You are not alone on this journey. God is your strength, your shield, and your deliverer. Your declarations are a testament to your faith and trust in His unchanging Word. With every word you speak, you align yourself with His will, paving the way for His blessings to flow freely into your life and the lives of those around you.

As you move forward, continue to make prophetic declarations a daily habit. Speak life over your family, community, and future. Watch as God's power is revealed in ways that exceed your expectations. Let this be your anthem as you step into the fullness of God's promises (Jeremiah 29:11): "For I know the thoughts that I think toward you, says the Lord, thoughts of peace and not of evil, to give you a future and a hope."

You have everything you need to walk confidently into the abundant life God has prepared for you. Take hold of it boldly, and let your decrees shape your destiny, glorify God, and transform the world around you.

As we conclude the journey of learning to decree with power and purpose, this chapter leaves you with an open invitation to embrace a lifestyle of confidence rooted in God's promises. Moving forward, you'll discover how to speak life and truth into every situation, allowing God's Word to shape your decisions, actions, and future with boldness and assurance.

Following this empowering chapter, the appendices provide a practical toolkit to support your ongoing journey. With comprehensive scriptural references, ready-to-use decree templates, and resources for further study, these final sections are designed to deepen your faith and equip you to overcome challenges with confidence. Together, they are a reminder that this is not the end but a new beginning—one filled with promise, power, and the transformative potential of God's Word spoken through your life.

Conclusion

As you reach the end of this book, take a moment to reflect on the transformative journey you've undertaken. Together, we've explored the biblical foundations, practical applications, and profound impact of prophetic decrees in your personal life, family, community, and beyond. You've learned to wield the power of God's Word with authority, standing on His promises to shape our reality and overcome every challenge.

Throughout these pages, key principles have been emphasized: the importance of aligning your words with God's truth, the necessity of speaking life over every situation, and the transformative potential of daily declarations. From overcoming opposition to experiencing restoration and revival, decrees are more than mere words, they are faith-filled proclamations that unleash divine power into your circumstances.

The Power of Prophetic Decrees

The journey began with understanding the biblical basis for prophetic decrees—diving into Scriptures that reveal God's design for His people to declare his truth boldly. You've seen how decrees align your heart and spirit with God's will, changing atmospheres and breaking strongholds.

Through real-life testimonies and biblical examples, you've witnessed the power of decrees in actions, restoring relationships, bringing healing, and catalyzing revival. You've explored practical steps to include declarations into your daily life, learning to speak protection, blessings, and favor over yourself and your loved ones.

The call to action remains simple yet profound; prophetic decrees are a regular part of your faith journey. Start small, using the templates and examples provided, and grow in confidence as you see God move in response to your words.

Call to Action

The next step is yours to take. Let this book be the beginning of a powerful new chapter in your life. Start today by identifying areas in your life that need transformation. Open your Bible, find Scriptures that speak to your situation, and craft declarations rooted in God's promises. Speak them aloud with faith and trust that God's Word will not return void.

Here are some practical steps to begin:

- **Set a daily routine:** Dedicate time each day to speak decrees over your life. Mornings are often ideal, as they set the tone for the day ahead.

- **Engage with Scripture:** Continue to dive into God's Word, searching for verses that resonate with your current needs and desires.

- **Record your journey:** Keep a journal of your declarations and the outcomes you witness. Testimonies of answered prayers will strengthen your faith and inspire others.

- **Share with others:** Encourage your family, friends, and community to join you in speaking prophetic decrees. The impact multiplies when believers unite in faith and purpose.

Initially, you may feel uncertain, but remember that God honors every step of faith, no matter how small. If you're unsure of where to begin, turn to the sample templates in the appendices. Let them guide you until you feel comfortable crafting your own. Trust that as you align your words with God's truth, you are planting seeds that will yield a harvest of blessings in due time.

You don't need to wait for the perfect moment or a grand revelation. Begin where you are with what you have. Speak life over your home, your health, your relationships, and your future. Speak protection over your family, wisdom over your decisions, and favor over your endeavors. Watch as God moves in ways that exceed your expectations.

Prayer of Dedication

Heavenly Father,

Thank You for the incredible journey You've led me on through this book. I dedicate myself to a life of speaking Your Word with boldness and faith. Teach me to align my heart, mind, and spirit with Your truth. Help me to grow in confidence as I decree Your promises over every area of my life. May my words always bring glory to You and align with Your perfect will.

I commit to using this tool of prophetic declarations as an act of faith, trusting that Your Word will accomplish all that You desire. Strengthen me, guide me, and empower me to walk in the fullness of Your plans for my life. In Jesus' name, I pray. Amen.

Final Prayer

Father,

I thank You for the truths revealed in this book. Seal them in my heart and mind so that I may walk forward in faith and confidence. I declare that Your Word is living and powerful, sharper than any two-edged sword, and I commit to using it to shape my life according to Your will.

Bless every reader who has embarked on this journey. Equip them with courage, wisdom, and perseverance as they step into the calling You've placed on their lives.

Let them see breakthroughs, miracles, and transformations as they faithfully declare Your promises.

Lord, let this be more than just words on a page—let it be a movement of Your Spirit, bringing revival, healing, and hope to individuals, families, and communities. We trust in Your power and stand on Your Word, believing that all things are possible through You. In Jesus' mighty name, we pray. Amen.

As you close this book, let it not mark the end but a powerful new beginning. You are now equipped with tools, truths, and testimonies to live your life marked by faith, purpose, and transformation. Go forth with confidence, knowing that God's Word in your mouth is as powerful as God's Word in his mouth.

May your journey be filled with joy, victory, and the unwavering assurance that God is for you. Speak boldly, live courageously, and watch as His promises unfold in your life. You are called, chosen, and empowered; now go and declare His glory to the world.

Appendices

The appendices are designed to serve as a practical resource hub for your journey with prophetic decrees. They provide tools, references, and further study opportunities to deepen your understanding and empower you to walk confidently in God's promises.

Practical Tips for Using These Resources

- Dedicate time to studying and meditating on the scriptures listed in Appendix A.

- Practice crafting personal decrees based on the examples in Appendix B.

- Explore the recommended books or websites in Appendix C during your devotional time to deepen your knowledge.

Appendix A: Scriptural References for Decrees

Scripture forms the foundation for every declaration you speak. When you align your word with God's Word, you activate the power and authority that comes from heaven. Below is a comprehensive list of

Bible verses you can use as a foundation for decrees in various areas of life.

Decrees for Protection

- Psalm 91:1–2: "He who dwells in the secret place of the Most High shall abide under the shadow of the Almighty. I will say of the Lord, 'He is my refuge and my fortress; My God, in Him I will trust.'"

- Isaiah 54:17: "No weapon formed against you shall prosper, and every tongue which rises against you in judgment You shall condemn."

- 2 Thessalonians 3:3: "But the Lord is faithful, and He will strengthen you and protect you from the evil one."

- Psalm 91:11: "For He will command His angels concerning you to guard you in all your ways."

Decrees for Provision

- Philippians 4:19: "And my God shall supply all your need according to His riches in glory by Christ Jesus."

- Deuteronomy 28:12: "The Lord will open to you His good treasure, the heavens, to give the rain to your land in its season and to bless all the work of your hand."

- Matthew 6:33: "But seek first His kingdom and His righteousness, and all these things will be given to you as well."

- Psalm 37:25: "I have been young, and now am old, yet I have not seen the righteous forsaken, or his descendants begging bread."

Decrees of Healing

- Exodus 15:26: "For I am the Lord who heals you."

- Isaiah 53:5: "By His stripes, we are healed."

- Psalm 34:18: "The Lord is close to the brokenhearted and saves those who are crushed in spirit."

- Isaiah 61:3: "To provide for those who grieve in Zion, to bestow on them a crown of beauty instead of ashes, the oil of joy instead of morning, and a garment of praise instead of a spirit of despair."

- Jeremiah 30:17: "But I will restore you to health and heal your wounds,' declares the Lord,"

Decrees for Family Unity

- Joshua 24:15: "As for me and my house, we will serve the Lord."

- Colossians 3:13: "Bear with each other and forgive one another if any of you has a grievance against someone."

- Ephesians 4:3: "Make every effort to keep the unity of the Spirit through the bond of peace."

- Psalm 133:1: "How good and pleasant it is when God's people live together in unity!"

Decrees for Overcoming Fear

- 2 Timothy 1:7: "For God has not given us a spirit of fear, but of power and of love and of a sound mind."

- Psalm 27:1: "The Lord is my light and my salvation; whom shall I fear?"

- Isaiah 41:10: "So do not fear, for I am with you; do not be dismayed, for I am your God. I will strengthen you and help you; I will uphold you with my righteous right hand."

- Philippians 4:13: "I can do all things through Christ who strengthens me."

Appendix B: Sample Decree Templates

To help you get started, here are ready-to-use templates for various situations. These templates are structured to guide you in declaring God's Word with clarity and confidence.

Decree for Financial Breakthrough

I decree and declare that the Lord is my provider. According to His Word (Philippians 4:19), all my needs are met according to His riches in glory. I am blessed in my coming and going (Deuteronomy 28:6), and the work of my hands is prospering (Psalm 1:3). Scarcity and debt have no hold over me. Abundance and provision are my portion in Jesus' name.

Decree for Physical Healing

I decree that by the stripes of Jesus, I am healed (Isaiah 53:5). Sickness and disease have no place in my body. I am fearfully and wonderfully made (Psalm 139:14), and every cell, tissue, and organ in my body aligns with God's perfect design. I declare health, wholeness, and restoration in Jesus' name.

Decree for Family Reconciliation

I decree that my family is united under the banner of God's love (1 Corinthians 13:7). Forgiveness flows freely among us, and peace reigns in our home (Colossians 3:15). We are a household that serves the Lord (Joshua 24:15). Love, respect, and understanding are restored in Jesus' name.

Decree for Victory in Spiritual Warfare

I decree that I am more than a conqueror through Christ (Romans 8:37). I put on the full armor of God (Ephesians 6:11) and stand firm against the scheme of the enemy. No weapon formed against me shall prosper (Isaiah 54:17). I declare victory in every battle in Jesus' name.

Decree for Spiritual Growth

I decree and declare that I am growing in wisdom, knowledge, and understanding of God's Word (Proverbs 2:6). My heart is receptive and my spirit is aligned with His truth. As I seek Him daily, He reveals mysteries and empowers me with His wisdom (Jeremiah 33:3). I am transformed by the renewing of my mind (Romans 12:2) and my life reflects His glory.

Decree for Overcoming Anxiety

I decree that I will not be anxious about anything, but in every situation, by prayer and petition, with thanksgiving, I present my requests to God (Philippians 4:6).

The peace of God, which transcends all understanding, guards my heart and mind in Christ Jesus (Philippians 4:7). I declare that fear and worry have no hold over me. I walk in peace, trusting in His perfect plan."

Decree for Workplace Success

I decree and declare that the work of my hand is blessed (Deuteronomy 28:12). I have the mind of Christ (1 Corinthians 2:16), and His wisdom guides me in every decision. Doors of opportunity are opening, and I walk boldly into the assignments God has prepared for me (Ephesians 2:10). Favor surrounds me like a shield (Psalm 5:12).

Decree for Nations and Communities

I decree and declare that righteousness exalts this nation (Proverbs 14:34). I speak peace, prosperity, and unity over our leaders and communities (1 Timothy 2:1-2).

Revival is stirring, and God's Kingdom is advancing in every sphere of influence. His will be done on earth as it is in heaven (Matthew 6:10).

Feel free to adapt these templates to fit your specific needs. The key is to personalize them with your unique circumstances while staying rooted in God's Word.

Appendix C: Resources for Future Study

Exploring prophetic decrees in greater depth can enrich your understanding and practice. Here are some recommended resources to guide you:

- **Books**

    o *Decree Your Today* by Patricia King. A practical guide to speaking life and blessings over your circumstances (Ministries, 2016).

    o *Power of Your Words* by E.W. Kenyon. Insights into the spiritual impact of spoken words (Gossett & Kenyon, 2021).

    o *The Prophetic Intercessor* by James W. Goll. A deeper dive into the power of prophetic prayer and declarations (Goll, 2007).

- **Websites**

    o *Bible Study Tools*: A comprehensive site for exploring Scripture and its applications.

- *Got Questions:* Biblically based answers to faith-related questions.

- *Charisma Magazine:* Articles and insights on prophetic ministry and declarations.

- **Podcasts and Sermons**

    - *The Prophetic Edge* by Shawn Bolz: Teachings on hearing God's voice and declaring His Word.

    - *Declarations of Faith* by Joseph Prince: Practical examples of speaking faith-filled decrees.

- **Bible Apps**

    - *YouVersion Bible App:* Offers tools for Scripture memorization and topical studies.

    - *Blue Letter Bible:* Features interlinear Bible tools and commentary for deeper study.

References

Ashcraft, S. (2019). *Repeat the sound of joy—Until it becomes a habit.* ChristianityToday.com. https://www.christianitytoday.com/

Azusa Street mission. (2024). Azusastreetmission. http://www.azusastreetmission.org/home0.aspx

The Azusa Street revival - 1906-1908. (n.d.). apostolicarchives https://www.apostolicarchives.com/articles/article/880192 5/173190.htm

Bethel Church | On earth as it is in heaven. (2019). Bethel.com. https://www.bethel.com/

Biwila, D. (2021, November). *No more migraine headaches. The Christian Science Journal.* https://journal.christianscience.com/issues/ 2021/11/139-11/no-more-migraine-headaches

Bofelo. (2024). *Case study 1: Emily's self-exploration.* Studocu.com. https://www.studocu.com/row/messages/question/348262

4/case-study-1-emilys-self-exploration-background-emily-is-a-28-year-old-woman-who-is

Brown, K. (2017, August 21). *Young woman's raw testimony of faith in the face of depression.* GodTube.com. https://www.godtube.com/blog/womans-raw-testimony-depression.html

CBN Europe. (2022). *Listen to Sarah's testimony in under 60 seconds about her journey of healing & restoration from addiction through the power of God.* https://www.facebook.com/watch/?v=5944616215605083

Frederickson, E. (2015). *Interview with Joe Turner by The Recovering Reality podcast.* Spotify for Creators. https://creators.spotify.com/pod/ show/erik-frederickson/episodes/interview-with-joe-turner-e30dvg

From rags to riches: real-life financial miracles that will leave you inspired. (n.d.). Exam Academy. https://tomdunnacademy.org/financial-miracles-testimonies/

Gilder, K. V. (2016, May 5). *Southern West Virginia revival rooted in prayer.* Billy Graham Evangelistic Association. https://billygraham.org/story/southern-west-virginia-revival-rooted-in-prayer/

GodUpdates. (2024). https://www.godupdates.com/page/2/

Goll, J. W. (2007). *The prophetic intercessor.* Chosen Books.

Gossett, D., & Kenyon, E. W. (2021, February 16). *The power of your words.* Audiobooks.com. https://www.audiobooks.com/ audiobook/power-of-your-words/503291?refid=40912&mscl kid=13edaae5005515ec9df1cd960c63a5b7

Green's, D. (2017, April 17). *Think eternity.* https://thinke.org/blog/your-legacy

Green, H. (2024). *Thinking, feeling, and believing - Case study – Susan: Adjusting career goals.* https://www.studocu.com/en-

us/document/capella-university/introduction-to-social-
psychology/thinking-feeling-and-believing/96043941

Gustafson, A. (2023, September 11). *Experiencing God changes us, Linda
    Morrison's story (Episode 68)*. Somebody Cares America.

https://somebodycares.org/experiencing-god-changes-us-linda-morrisons-story-episode-68/

A healing confession. (2013, September 17). CBN. https://cbn.com/article/not-selected/healing-confession

Johnson, B. (n.d.). *Guideposts.* https://guideposts.org/

Lawrence, A. (2024). *From hopelessness to city of hope.* Prayerleader.com. https://www.prayerleader.com/from-hopelessness-to-city-of-hope/?print=print

Lisa Whittle. (2024). FaithGateway. https://faithgateway.com/collections/lisa-whittle

Living Faith Church Worldwide. (2023, November 14). *Striking testimonies: Barrenness terminated via prophetic declaration.* YouTube. https://www.youtube.com/watch?v=ybrnaahvrgi

Marshall, S. (2018, March). *17 true inspirational stories of real-life overcomers.* Salem Web Network. https://www.godtube.com/blog/true-inspirational-stories-overcomers.html

Ministries, P. K. (2016). *Decree 3rd edition.* Patricia King Ministries. https://store.patriciakingministries.com/products/decree-book-3rd-edition-by-patricia-king-2?variant=34816199689

New King James Version. (2017). Bible Gateway. https://www.biblegateway.com/passage/?search=numbers%206%3a22-27&version=nkjv

1995 Cali, Colombia revival. (2021, September 2). Beautiful Feet. https://romans1015.com/cali/

Osteen, D. (2019). *If my heart could talk.* Lakewoodchurch.com. https://www.lakewoodchurch.com/store/products/dcb000 3e

Osteen, D. (2023, May 30). *Dodie Osteen testimony.* Word for Life Publishing. https://wordforlifepublishing.com/dodie-osteen-testimony/

Papaleontiou-Louca, E. (2021). Effects of religion and faith on mental health. *New Ideas in Psychology, 60,* 100833. https://doi.org/10.1016/j.newideapsych.2020.100833

Prince, J. (2024). *Praise report - restored mother-daughter relationship.* Joseph Prince Ministries. https://www.josephprince.org/blog/praise-reports/restored-mother-daughter-relationship?utm_source=chatgpt.com

Rachel. (2024). *The desperate mother*. Rayfowler.org. https://www.rayfowler.org/sermons/famous-mothers-in-the-bible/rachel-the-desperate-mother/

Sara. (2022, July 29). *Should a Christian use positive affirmations?* The Holy Mess. https://theholymess.com/christian-positive-affirmations/

Save my marriage testimonies. (2013, April 1). Marriage Missions International. https://marriagemissions.com/about-us-2/save-my-marriage-testimonies-3/

Share, T. (2009, February 17). *Testimony share – God healed me from anxiety and depression*. https://testimonyshare.com/god-healed-me-from-anxiety-and-depression/

Smith, D. (2018, November 14). *Church becomes a refuge in California's devastating fire*. OpentheWord.org. https://opentheword.org/

2018/11/14/church-becomes-a-place-of-refuge-in-californias-devastating-fire/

Stevens, P. (2017, June 20). *The life of George Muller*. GeorgeMuller.org. https://www.georgemuller.org/devotional/the-life-of-george-muller

VertexValue. (2024, December 5). *The struggling business owner: A success story*. YouTube. Https://www.youtube.com/watch?v=2oxvhhedxso

Williams, J. (2024). *Understanding the Williams Family: Exploring complexities*. Coursehero.com. https://www.coursehero.com/file/224515638/personal-family-genogramdocx/

Printed in Dunstable, United Kingdom

67269303R00107